$10.00

IT HAPPENED IN THE REVOLUTIONARY WAR

It Happened In Series

IT HAPPENED IN THE REVOLUTIONARY WAR

Michael R. Bradley

TWODOT®

GUILFORD, CONNECTICUT
HELENA, MONTANA

AN IMPRINT OF THE GLOBE PEQUOT PRESS

A · TWODOT® · BOOK

Library of Congress Cataloging-in-Publication Data

Bradley, Michael R. (Michael Raymond). 1940-

It happened in the Revolutionary War / Michael R. Bradley.—1st ed.

p.cm. — (It happened in series)

"A TwoDot book"—T.p. verso.

Includes bibliographical references and index.

ISBN 0-7627-2215-0

1. United States—History--Revolution, 1775–1783—Anecdotes.

I. Title. II. Series.

E296 .B74 2003

973.3—dc21 200209495

Manufactured in the United States of America

First Edition/First Printing

I honor William Bradley, who fought and was wounded at Kings Mountain. I am glad the wound was not fatal, or I would not be here to write this.

Contents

Preface

There was once a time when giants walked abroad in this land. All of us who are citizens of the United States, anyone, anywhere who loves liberty, is their descendant.

They were not perfect, those men and women of the Revolutionary War era. Some of them were fearful, some were self seeking, some wavered in their devotion to the cause of freedom. But they produced a nation that has become a beacon set on a hill, beckoning to all who want to walk toward freedom. The nation those men and women produced has not been, and is not, a perfect nation, but millions of Americans would prefer to awake no place else.

In this book you will meet some of the people of that Revolutionary age: men, women, even children, of all races, some of whom measured up to the challenge of birthing a nation and some who failed in the attempt to do their share. We can take pride in those who were patriots, and we can learn even from those who failed.

In this book the word *American* is not often used. During the Revolutionary War, "American" was used to designate any resident of any of the British colonies in North America, including Canada and the Caribbean. "American" referred to a place of residence, not citizenship. When the war began, everyone in the colonies was British so far as citizenship was concerned. A new meaning for the word *American* had to be invented. While our ancestors were inventing that meaning, they called themselves "Patriots" and the army the "Continentals." The British called us "Rebels" and other things totally unfit for print. Only gradually did *American* come to denote a citizen of the United States and a certain set of political ideals.

The original thirteen states were not strongly united either. At the same time that they declared their independence from

Great Britain, the Continental Congress drew up, and submitted to the states for ratification, a document called the Articles of Confederation. Under the terms of this agreement, each state retained its sovereignty, and practically no power was given to the central government. Our original national government was a states' rights confederacy. As a result of this form of government, the treaty ending the Revolutionary War was not negotiated between Great Britain and the United States of America but between Britain and thirteen sovereign entities, each listed in the treaty by name. Not until 1789 did we alter this arrangement between the states and national government by writing the Constitution of the United States of America, one purpose of which was "to create a more perfect union."

Whether your ancestors helped found Jamestown, stubbed their toe on Plymouth Rock, came ashore on Ellis Island, or arrived just the other day, the men and women of this book are your political ancestors. They helped give us what we have as Americans.

Revolutionary War Timeline

1754 — Albany Conference takes place. Colonies reject a proposal by Benjamin Franklin suggesting that all colonies cooperate in self-defense against the French and Indians.

1754–1761 — French and Indian War, also called the Seven Years' War, causes havoc for the colonists. French and Indians attack the colonial frontier. Most of the defense of the colonies is provided by the colonial militia.

1762–1763 — Chief Pontiac leads what will become known as Pontiac's Rebellion, causing the British government to forbid white settlement west of the Appalachian Mountains

1764 — Parliament passes the Sugar Act, placing a tax on molasses, a commodity vital to New England. The New England colonies distill the molasses into the rum that is taken to Africa to be traded for slaves, who are in turn taken to the Caribbean to be traded for more molasses.

1765 — Stamp Act requires a revenue stamp on all sorts of documents, thus creating yet more taxes.

1766 — In the face of colonial opposition, the British Parliament repeals the Sugar and Stamp Acts.

1767 Parliament imposes the Townshend Duties, a tax on paint, paper, lead, glass, and tea. This tax is paid in Britain by the exporter, but the colonists know they will have the tax passed on to them in the form of higher prices.

1768 Violent antitax protests break out in Boston and other towns. Troops are sent to Boston to maintain order.

1770 The Boston Massacre occurs when British troops fire on an unruly crowd. Four citizens of Boston are killed.

1771 Troops are withdrawn from Boston, and the Townshend Duties are repealed, except for the tax on tea.

1773 A bumper crop of tea makes that item a bargain even with the tax. The Sons of Liberty in Boston dump tea overboard in what becomes known as the Boston Tea Party.

Parliament passes the Intolerable Acts to punish Boston.

1774 British troops return to Boston to maintain order.

1775 War officially begins on April 19 at Lexington and Concord, Massachusetts; Minutemen besiege Boston.

Battle of Bunker Hill takes place.

George Washington is made commander of the Continental Army.

Siege of Boston continues.

1776	Henry Knox brings cannons to Boston from Fort Ticonderoga.
	British army evacuates Boston. Washington moves the Continental Army to New York City.
	British attack Charleston, South Carolina, and are defeated.
	Colonies declare independence.
	Washington is defeated at New York City, and the Patriot army loses heavily in men and material.
	Battle of Trenton takes place.
1777	Battle of Princeton takes place.
	Battle of Brandywine Creek takes place. The British capture Philadelphia, the Patriot capital.
	Washington retreats to Valley Forge.
	A Patriot force at Saratoga, New York, forces a British army led by Gen. John Burgoyne to surrender.
1778	Gen. Wilhelm von Steuben trains the Continental Army at Valley Forge.
	Battle of Monmouth Courthouse takes place. The Continental Army stands its ground in the open field for the first time. The war in the north comes to a stalemate—Washington's men are in New Jersey, and the British are in New York City.

1779	British attempt to overrun the southern colonies.
	Savannah, Georgia, is captured by the British.
	Augusta, Georgia is captured by the British.
1780	Charleston, South Carolina, is captured by the British.
	Battle of Camden takes place. The Patriots are defeated.
	Battle of Kings Mountain takes place. The Patriot forces win.
1781	Patriots win the Battle of Cowpens.
	Siege of Yorktown takes place. Lord Cornwallis is forced to surrender to Washington when the British fleet is turned back by the French at the mouth of Chesapeake Bay.
	Peace negotiations begin.
1782	Patriot forces fighting in the South continue to take back British-controlled territory; peace negotiations are on-going.
1783	Congress ratifies the Treaty of Paris on April 19, ending the war exactly eight years after it began.

Martyrs of a Massacre or Victims of a Propaganda Ploy?

On March 5, 1770, four men were shot dead by British soldiers on the streets of Boston and four more were wounded in what would later be called the Boston Massacre. Were these men the first martyrs to the cause of independence or were they the victims of a clever propaganda ploy?

By 1768 relations between some segments of the colonial population and the British authorities had become so strained that violence frequently broke out. The heart of the controversy was whether the Parliament in London had the authority to levy taxes on the colonies or whether that power rested in the hands of the legislatures of each colony. Beginning with the Sugar Act of 1764 and the Stamp Act of 1765, Parliament asserted its right, and the colonies stoutly asserted theirs through various acts of defiance. In its latest action Parliament had placed taxes on lead, paint, paper, glass, and tea. Leading the colonial opposition was a secret organization called the Sons of Liberty. Men who had taken a stand on both sides of the issue were beaten or doused in tar and feathers; windows were broken and buildings were burned. From the perspective of the Royal government, the behavior of some Americans had degenerated to the level of unruly children engaged in a temper tantrum. The governor of Massachusetts, Thomas Hutchinson, found it necessary to ask for troops to be sent to Boston to keep order. Already his house had been attacked and his family had been threatened.

The requested troops came in impressive numbers. From Ireland came the Sixty-fourth and Sixty-fifth Infantry Regiments, while the Fourteenth and Twenty-ninth arrived in Nova Scotia along with a company of artillery armed with five cannons. Because Boston was a town of only 18,000 population at the time, this was a heavy military presence.

For two years the troops were quartered in and around Boston, and for two years tensions between soldiers and townspeople increased. There were fights between soldiers and civilians over girls, brawls in taverns when too much beer had been consumed, and conflicts when off-duty soldiers took on part-time jobs, depriving local men of work. And there was the biggest issue of all: The soldiers were the living symbol of the authority Parliament claimed to control and tax the colonies.

Of course the local members of the Sons of Liberty took advantage of every clash between townspeople and soldiers to stir up more resentment and to make yet more trouble. Because the leader of the Sons of Liberty was assumed to be Samuel Adams, and because Sam ran a brewery, a crowd of Sons could easily be gathered and moved to action by a few pints of beer.

March 5, 1770, dawned cold and snowy. The bad weather kept many of those who worked out-of-doors away from their jobs. Not surprisingly, many of these men congregated in the taverns around town to chat, keep warm, and drink. All during that day, it was later recorded, a mysterious man identified only as "tall, and wearing a red cloak" made his way around the taverns making inflammatory speeches about the British presence in Boston.

By dark there was almost a foot of snow on the streets of Boston, but the military routine of the British army followed its normal course, posting guards at strategic locations around town. Pvt. Hugh White of the Twenty-ninth Regiment was placed on duty at the Custom House. This building was a symbol of the Crown's authority in Boston, because it was from the Custom House that the hated tax laws were enforced.

At about eight o'clock that night, a group of townspeople began moving down King Street. To all who would listen, they said some soldiers had attacked them, and they were getting clubs and going to find some Redcoat on whom they could take their revenge. As this crowd approached the Custom House, another group, which included children, was gathering at the barracks occupied by the soldiers. There was a good deal of swearing and shouting, and the officers had a lot of trouble keeping their men from wading into the crowd with guns and bayonets.

Church bells began to ring, usually a signal that a house was on fire, and more people came pouring into the street. As the crowd in front of him grew in size, Pvt. Hugh White began to feel decidedly lonely. Many in the mob were armed with clubs, and most of the rest had begun to lob snowballs at him. Convinced he could not control the situation, Private White did just what army regulations said he should do: He called for the officer of the day.

Capt. Thomas Preston had a reputation as a good officer who stayed calm in a crisis. Preston decided to send six privates under Cpl. William Wemms to assist Private White. Because of the delicacy of the situation, Captain Preston followed this relief force himself.

Reaching the besieged private, Captain Preston decided the situation was too dangerous to return to the main guard post. Instead, he formed his little band into a semicircle with their backs to the entrance to the Custom House. In an attempt to cow the crowd, Preston ordered his men to load their guns. Instead of making the crowd afraid, this move made them more bold.

The crowd knew that the soldiers were under regulations that did not allow them to take action against civilians without orders from a civil official. Because no one was present to give such an order, they pressed right up against the bayonets of the soldiers, challenging them to fire. The crowd had forgotten one basic rule: Under the Common Law of Britain, no one was denied the right of self-defense when faced with a deadly attack.

A club came whirling out of the crowd and struck Pvt. Hugh Montgomery, knocking him down. Getting back on his feet, Montgomery fired. So did all the other soldiers. Four men fell to the ground, dead; four others were wounded. The dead were Samuel Gray, James Caldwell, Samuel Maverick, and Michael Johnson, who was also known as Crispus Attucks and was of mixed Native American and African ancestry. He is often called the nation's first African American hero.

The British soldiers were brought to trial in later weeks, but the court found they had acted in self-defense. The lawyer for the soldiers had secretly been hired by the Sons of Liberty, who wanted the men acquitted as an indicator that more had to be done about the issue. The four dead men became martyrs to those who were pressing for independence. But they may also have been victims of a propaganda ploy that was designed to stir up trouble and, in the soldiers' retaliation, brought them more than they had bargained for.

Before Lexington and Concord: The Real First Shots

By the rude bridge that arched the flood . . .
Here once the embattled farmers stood
And fired the shot heard round the world.

So said Ralph Waldo Emerson in his well-known poem "Concord Hymn." Following the message of that poem, and the contents of dozens of books, the majority of contemporary Americans would agree that the opening shots of the Revolutionary War were fired early on the morning of April 19, 1775, at Lexington and Concord in Massachusetts.

But were they? Historians readily admit that which the public does not know—that the first confrontation between armed forces of the Crown and the colonies occurred five months before Lexington and Concord and in another colony. Emerson would have needed all his literary ability to write a poem about the event, however. It occurred on December 14 and 15, 1774, at Fort William and Mary in the harbor of Portsmouth, New Hampshire.

The year 1774 was a time of rising tension between Britain and the American colonies. Since 1761 the Parliament of Great Britain had been attempting to assess taxes to be paid in the colonies. The purpose of these taxes was to pay the debts incurred by Britain during the Seven Years' War (1754–1761) with France. Britain, and her North American colonies, had benefited enormously from the war. When the conflict began, France was a major force in North America; at its conclusion there was no French territory left on the continent. Britain figured the colonies should be willing to help pay for the military effort that had eliminated the major allies of the Indians. But all their attempts to tax had been met with resistance. The colonies were accustomed to levying taxes on themselves, not to having someone far away do so. The slogan of the colonists became, "No taxation without representation." They were willing to pay taxes, but only those in whose levying they had a direct voice.

Eventually, all the taxes passed by Parliament were repealed except for the levy on tea. In 1773 resistance to this remaining tax led to the Boston Tea Party, during which a group of colonists dumped overboard all the tea aboard the ship *Dartmouth*. In the face of this destruction of private property, the British government began to take stern measures to bring the colonies to obedience. These measures included sending troops to Boston, the major trouble spot, and continuing the efforts to export tea, tax and all, to America. In response, the colonies formed "Committees of Correspondence" to coordinate their resistance.

In Portsmouth, New Hampshire, the Committee of Correspondence was headed by Samuel Cutts, a leading merchant. On July 4, 1774, twenty-seven chests of tea arrived in Portsmouth. The British government apparently had decided to determine if they could have better luck selling tea, and collecting taxes, in Portsmouth than they had had in Boston. The local Committee of Correspondence promptly pressured the recipient to send the tea on to the port of Halifax in Canada, and soon it was on its way. This quiet method of opposition was much more widespread among the colonists than was the spectacular direct challenge given to the tea tax in Boston.

Not long after, in defiance of the orders of the Royal Governor, Thomas Wentworth, delegates were elected to the Continental Congress. This was not a legislative body and had no official governmental authority. Yet every colony was represented in the Congress. Instead of being merely a protest meeting, the Continental Congress became the de facto government of America. Because the Congress was organizing military units—the Minutemen—the king ordered that no gunpowder or other military goods be shipped to the colonies.

This last action roused a local Portsmouth Patriot leader, John Sullivan, to action. "I took the alarm, clearly perceiving the design of the British ministry, and wrote several pieces on the necessity of securing military stores which were published in several papers." Sullivan then began to plan his next move. By December 2, 1774, Governor Wentworth sensed a growing "unrest and a disposition of the people to follow all the Resolves of the Congress."

Then Paul Revere rode into town. On December 13 Revere delivered to Samuel Cutts a letter from the Boston Committee of Correspondence saying that troops were being sent to reinforce the garrison of Fort William and Mary at the mouth of Portsmouth Harbor. This information was incorrect, but the letter also contained the news that the British had seized military stores in Rhode Island and were planning to do the same in all the colonies. Such was, indeed, the British policy.

Revere's letter touched off a furor in the town of Portsmouth. During the morning of December 14, a drummer marched all around town beating the call to assemble. By noon people from the adjacent towns of Newcastle and Rye were streaming into town. The governor sent an official to order the crowd to disperse, but this had no effect. By one o'clock a crowd numbering 400 was marching on the fort.

Inside the walls of the fort, Capt. John Cochran could muster only five men to defend the post. As the crowd approached the fort he ordered them to stop. As the group surged closer, Cochran "immediately ordered three four-pounders to fire on them, and then the small arms." Before the garrison could reload, they had been overrun. No one had been hit. Captain Cochran and his men were locked up for about ninety minutes while the crowd broke into the powder magazine and ran off with one hundred barrels of gunpowder.

On December 15 John Sullivan marched into town at the head of men he had assembled. Sullivan was pleased that the powder had been taken, but he knew much of value remained in the fort. Leading his men into the now empty fortification, he seized sixty muskets and cartridge boxes and sixteen of the lighter-weight cannons. These, along with the powder, were loaded on large rowboats and taken up the Durham River to be dispersed and hidden throughout the countryside. All day on December 16, a guard of New Hampshire men occupied the town as the ice in the river was cut to open a channel. The rowboats slowly disappeared upstream. John Sullivan paid the expenses of gathering the boats and equipment out of his own pocket. Eleven years later Congress voted to repay him one hundred dollars for his patriotic service.

Persistent, and plausible, folklore accounts say some of the gunpowder was hidden under the pulpit of the Durham town church, while a cartload was shipped to Boston, where it was used against the British at Bunker Hill.

Two ships of the Royal Navy, the *Scarborough* and the *Canceaux*, arrived to assist the fort on December 17, but they were too late. The powder and weapons were safely in the interior of the colony. And the first shots of the Revolutionary War had been fired.

Turning an Insult Against the Insulter

Yankee Doodle went to town
A-riding on a pony,
Stuck a feather in his hat
And called it macaroni.

These words are known to millions of people, not just in the United States, but around the world. They are a part of one of the most famous of all American patriotic songs. The song is even the official song of the State of Connecticut. But who, or what, is a Yankee Doodle, what town is his destination, and why does he have pasta attached to his headgear? The answers are both obscure and interesting.

The source of the tune to which the words are sung is not known, and no scholarly research seems able to pin down the origin. Some researchers have suggested a Spanish dance as the original inspiration, but others have looked to Dutch peasant songs, French work songs, Basque melodies, or Irish tunes. The nearest melody in English musicology is a nursery rhyme called "Lucy Locket." Whatever the source, the tune was played by the British army during the French and Indian War (1754–1761).

The first word in the title—*Yankee*—is also of obscure origin. The Dutch, the first European settlers in New York, may well have set in motion the evolution of the word by calling their English neighbors "Jankee," the diminutive of Jan or John. However, the reverse may be true since the English sometimes called the Dutch "John Cheese" (Jan Kase) because of their round faces. Other possibilities for the origin of the term are *eankke* from the Iroquoian language, meaning "coward," or the Gaelic term *Yankie*, meaning a "shrewd woman." At any rate when Yankee came to be applied to the residents of the New England area, it did not have a positive meaning.

Doodle was also a derogatory term dating to the English Civil War of the seventeenth century. At that time the King's supporters dubbed the leading general on the Parliamentary side, Oliver Cromwell, "Doodle," because that was a nickname he had carried since his student days. Cromwell's reputation as a strict, humorless man did not endear him to later generations.

As the seventeenth century drew to a close the leading arbiter of fashion among European nobility, and those who copied the style of the nobility, was the Maccaroni family of Italy. These fashion trendsetters popularized a fancy, multi-feathered hat that became all the rage among the rich and famous of the day. Soon the hat had taken on the name of the family and was known as a "Maccaroni."

These various strands came together in America in 1754 when Britain went to war with France. This was only one in a series of conflicts that happened between 1701 and 1815. The root cause of all these wars was a struggle over colonial territory and a desire for world trade domination. The 1754 war, properly called the Seven Years' War, was the first of the conflicts to take place, in part, on the North American continent and to involve the English colonists. The British soldiers who were sent to America to fight the French in Canada did not think very highly of the militia units the colonies called up to help in the war effort.

This lack of respect was galling to the colonials who defended the frontier against the French and their Indian allies after the regulars of the Royal Army under Gen. Edward

Braddock blundered into an ambush that almost wiped out the British force. That the colonial militia succeeded where the regulars had failed made no difference. A soldier had to look the part, and the militia were seedy in appearance.

It is thought that a British surgeon named Dr. Richard Shuckburgh decided to write some mocking verses about these militiamen, and he set them to a well-known folk tune. Given the British habit of looking down on colonials, the song was soon popular throughout the Royal army. The poor colonial rode a pony, not a stallion, which would have been a proper warhorse. The rube went splashing along a muddy road just as if he were going to London, which, of course, he had never even seen. To top it off, the hick thought a chicken feather stuck in his cap was the height of fashion.

The tune became popular enough that it was used in a comic opera, *The Disappointment*, as early as 1767. British troops sent to Boston to enforce the unpopular tax laws used the song frequently to send a not-so-subtle message of superiority to the Bostonians.

When the Patriots dared to begin organizing military units and to gather supplies to oppose the laws imposed on them by Parliament, a British military expedition was sent out from Boston on April 18, 1775, to seize these supplies. After marching in secret during the night, the band accompanying the expedition struck up "Yankee Doodle" as they marched toward the village of Lexington and the first pitched battle of the war. The British were still using the song as an insult to the Patriot forces when they made their assault on Bunker Hill in June 1775. The fierceness of the Patriot defense of that position gave the British second thoughts, however, and the song dropped out of the repertoire of British bands.

But the American Patriots had not forgotten the taunts and insults of their opponents. As the war continued and the Patriots began to win, a version of the song appeared that described a visit by a father and son to the camp of Gen. George Washington.

Father and I went down to camp,

Along with Captain Gooding;

And there we saw the men and boys,

As thick as hasty pudding.

The verses describe the artillery and soldiers of the army.

Then came Yorktown. As the proud, but defeated, army of Gen. Lord Charles Cornwallis negotiated its surrender in September 1781, one of the details covered in the capitulation document said that the British would have to play one of their own marches as their troops marched out from their fortifications to lay down their arms. It was specifically stated that "Yankee Doodle" was not a British march. It was no great surprise to the British, given the history of the tune, that the Patriots would wish to ban the song. So the British troops marched out to the popular song "The World Turned Upside Down."

After their arms were piled and flags were furled, the British turned to march back to their lines as prisoners. As the columns of defeated men formed up, the bands of the victors, as was the custom of the time, struck up one of their songs.

The Patriot bands played "Yankee Doodle." The insult had been turned against the insulter.

How Well Could the Minutemen Shoot?

One of the most beloved myths of the American Revolution is that of the Minuteman, the volunteer soldier who left his plow standing in the furrow while he marched off with his neighbors to shoot down the Redcoats with unerring aim. This canny warrior concealed himself behind any available scrap of cover to enhance his ability to fight, while the clueless British stupidly wore brightly colored coats and stood in neat lines while waiting to be shot down.

Unfortunately, this view of the volunteer Patriot soldier is indeed a myth. Very few men ever belonged to the organization called "Minutemen," and those who did were not noted for marksmanship. In October 1774 the Massachusetts Assembly authorized the formation of special militia units that would include men who would respond to an alarm in "a minute's notice." These organizations were disbanded in April 1775 when the assembly authorized the formation of an army of 18,000 men who would serve for eight months. The name Minutemen was only in use for seven months. At the opening skirmishes at Lexington and Concord, there were 3,763 Minutemen present. If it is assumed that they fired an average of eighteen shots each from the time the fighting began just at sunup until the fracas ended at dark, then the Patriot forces fired 75,000 shots. In the process they hit only 273 British soldiers, or one hit for about each 300 shots fired. Although the Minutemen, and other Patriot forces, did fight from behind cover, these tactics were usually not effective. It was not until the Continental soldiers learned traditional European linear tactics, including how to deliver a bayonet charge, that they able to defeat the Royal Army.

Another legend says the Minutemen were adequate as soldiers but were hampered in their efforts because they were armed with technologically inferior weapons. The smoothbore muskets with which the men were armed are often pictured as so grossly inaccurate as to be more dangerous to the person firing them than they were to the person being fired at. This is also a myth. Both sides had more or less the same weapons.

The shoulder weapon commonly used by both sides during the Revolutionary War is properly called a smoothbore, muzzle-loading, flintlock musket. All were single-shot weapons that had to be reloaded after each discharge. Smoothbore means the inside of the barrel is smooth. A rifle is called a rifle because the inside of the barrel has grooves (rifling) cut into the metal. When the weapon is fired, these grooves cause the bullet to spin, giving a rifle greater accuracy and range. Because the inside of the barrel has no grooves, a smoothbore is less accurate than a rifle and doesn't have its range, but the smoothbore weapon could be manufactured easily using eighteenth-century technology, unlike rifles, which were slow and difficult to produce.

The musket is called "muzzle loading" because each time the weapon is loaded the gunpowder and shot must be poured into the muzzle of the gun and then rammed tightly into the breech with a ramrod.

The ignition mechanism of the musket is called the "lock." It consists of a small, hollowed out piece of metal called the "pan," which is attached to the side of the barrel and connected to the inside of the breech by a small hole through the metal of the barrel. A piece of metal called a "frizzen" is snapped down over the pan, and a set of jaws (the "cock") is positioned to strike the frizzen with a piece of flint when the trigger is pulled. The cock is powered by a spring.

To load his weapon a soldier on either side in the Revolutionary War held his musket in his left hand. With his right hand he reached into a leather cartridge box, which was worn slung from his left shoulder to his right side, and withdrew a paper cylinder that contained the proper amount of powder and a lead ball. Raising the cylinder to his mouth, the soldier used his teeth to tear open the paper cartridge. The lead ball was often held in the soldier's mouth while a little powder was poured into the pan and the frizzen was snapped down to hold it in place. The rest of the powder was then poured down the barrel, the bullet was spat into the muzzle, and the crumpled paper of the cartridge pushed in on top. The whole mass was then tamped down the length of the barrel with the ramrod and firmly seated at the breech, just opposite the tiny hole that connected with the pan.

Once this cumbersome loading process was complete, the soldier was ready to fire. Bringing the musket to his shoulder, he pulled back the cock containing the jaws clamping a piece of flint and pulled the trigger. The cock sprang forward, driven by the spring; the flint struck the steel of the frizzen, uncovering the pan and allowing sparks from the impact of flint on steel to fall into the gunpowder in the pan; the fire flashed from the pan into the breech, setting off the main charge; and the gun fired—sometimes.

Wind might blow the powder out of the pan; rain, snow, or fog might make the powder too damp; the flint might fail to throw off a spark; or the tiny hole connecting the pan to the interior of the breech might become obstructed. The amazing fact is that a trained musketman could load and fire his weapon three times in a minute, with some experts able to load and fire six shots per minute.

The musket issued to the British forces and carried by the Minutemen at the beginning of the war was called the Brown Bess. The design for this weapon had been developed during the reign of Queen Elizabeth I, and the barrel was finished in a brown color, hence the name. There had been improvements in the ignition system since the time of "Good Queen Bess," but the weapon had always had a .75-caliber bore and fired a .69-caliber ball. The difference between the diameter of the bore and the diameter of the ball was called "windage." The windage made the Brown Bess easy to load, because the ball would literally fall down the barrel to the breech, but the lack of a snug fit caused the flight of the bullet to be somewhat erratic, especially at a range of more than 75 or 80 yards.

During the course of the war, imports caused most of the Patriot forces to be equipped with the French Charleyville musket, which was .69-caliber and fired a .65-caliber ball. With less windage, this weapon was somewhat more accurate than the Brown Bess.

The Minuteman's modern reputation as an inaccurate shot has more to do with his training than with the technology of the weapon. Soldiers were not trained to pick and to fire at individual targets but to fire at the mass formation of the enemy directly in front of them. Battles were not won by accurate gunfire but by delivering enough fire that the enemy ranks were disordered. At the moment the disorder became evident, a bayonet charge would be delivered, and the shaken ranks of the enemy could not withstand it. The Minuteman was not expected to be a good shot, nor was he ever trained to be a marksman. The Minuteman was taught to load and fire as rapidly as possible and then to charge home with his bayonet. Ultimately, his musket was to be transformed into a spear when the bayonet was attached. Lacking bayonets in the early days of the war, the Minuteman never had a chance to develop into a truly effective battlefield operative.

The Pen Is Mightier Than the Sword

"These are the times that try men's souls. . . ." If one was a supporter of the Patriot cause, these words were literally true that early winter of 1776. The light of liberty was flickering, threatening to go out, leaving only a dark void where bright hopes had once shined. Earlier, in July, buoyed on a wave of optimism as the British evacuated Boston, the colonies had declared their independence from England, stating that "they were, and of right ought to be, free and independent states." Since then the cause of freedom had steadily declined as military disaster after disaster had plagued the army led by George Washington in battles around New York City. Now, that important seaport was lost, and the once-proud Patriot army of 17,000 had been reduced to a third of that number. The enlistments of the remaining members were to expire on the last day of the year, and no one stood ready to take their places.

Then, like a thunderclap, there appeared a pamphlet called *The Crisis*, which quickly was reprinted throughout the colonies. This publication, the first in a series eventually numbering thirteen, began with the stirring words: "These are the times that try men's souls. The summer soldier and the sunshine patriot will, in this crisis, shrink from the service of their country; but he that stands it *now*, deserves the love and thanks of man and woman." Like a hot iron these words seared their way into the conscience of an infant nation.

The author of these words, Thomas Paine, had been in the colonies only since November 30, 1774, but he had arrived with a radical zeal for independence already burning in his heart. That fire would help ignite a continentwide conflagration.

Thomas Paine was born in Thetford, England, in 1737, the son of a Quaker corsetmaker. After only a basic education, Paine married in 1759, only to be left a widower at the birth of a premature child. A second marriage a few years later failed badly, and Paine was anxious to distance himself from his alienated wife. Paine was also trying to get away from a job he hated. Ironically, Paine was a tax collector for the Crown. In this position Paine said he saw "into the numerous and various distresses of ordinary people." These "distresses" included falling wages, rising prices, and occasional food riots. Not content to merely observe, Paine became active in church activities that promoted relief for the needy, but he soon realized the problem was larger than religious resources could solve. At some point in this search for a better life, Thomas Paine met Benjamin Franklin, because in 1774 Franklin gave Paine letters of introduction to political leaders in Pennsylvania. Paine soon came to America. Within a few months he had become editor of the *Pennsylvania Magazine*, acquiring a forum in which to sound his views.

The outbreak of the Revolutionary War gave Paine the opportunity he wanted. His political views had long favored limiting Royal power, and independence for the colonies was the perfect cause to achieve that end. Not all his new countrymen saw the issue in those terms, however. While many were upset with the attempts of the British Parliament and the appointed Royal governors to run colonial affairs, most saw themselves as loyal to King George III, the leader of the most free and liberal government on earth. This vast majority of the population held to this idea even after fighting broke out.

Paine took on the task of persuading his new countrymen to seek more freedom from the Crown in his widely published pamphlet, *Common Sense.* In trenchant arguments Paine gave a scathing indictment of rule by kings and celebrated the blessings to be found when people ruled. In one forceful passage he wrote: "Of more worth is one honest man to society, and in the sight of God, than all the crowned ruffians that ever lived." Paine went on to advocate a democratic system of government with frequent elections and a written constitution. In a single stroke Paine made the idea of independence the central focus of the political debate. It was not government corruption that plagued America, he wrote, nor was it a coalition of evil department heads; America's problem was the monarchical system of government. As Paine's message spread, "common sense passed through the continent like an electric spark," according to one contemporary. Perhaps as many as 500,000 copies of *Common Sense* were distributed.

In the dark days of 1776, Paine would step into the breach a second time. Unlike most political writers who addressed themselves to the upper classes, assuming only they would be interested in or capable of understanding their arguments, Paine wrote to the common people: the soldiers whose enlistments were almost up, the militiamen who were reluctant to take the field, the wives and mothers hesitant to let their husbands and sons leave home. The force of Paine's arguments was reinforced by his actions. He did not write *The Crisis* while seated comfortably at a desk in a warm office. Shortly after independence was declared in July, he had joined a militia company. During the retreat from New York City, Paine had served as an aide to Gen. Nathanael Greene and was currently a part of Washington's army.

The public response to Paine's second pamphlet was again large and positive. Washington had *The Crisis* read to every company in his army, while state representatives in the Continental Congress had it republished and sent back to their home states. *The Crisis* appealed to the sense of duty that had been deeply instilled into many American minds by the religious heritage of Calvinism, the dominant theological view of the colonial period. It stuck at their sense of shame by implying that they were giving up the task because it was difficult, though the need to continue the work was obvious. It might be argued that the pamphlet, which appeared on December 23, 1776, did not win the upcoming battles of Washington's Winter Campaign, but it was a great help. Enough men responded to Paine's call to allow Washington to go on the offensive at the Trenton and Princeton battles, keeping the American Revolution alive and leading, at long last, to victory.

The war was fought with muskets, but without the will to take up arms, there would have been no American victory. During some of the most depressing days of the war, Thomas Paine supplied that will. If not mightier than the sword, the pen was an effective, and necessary, partner.

It Took a Good Snow

George Washington and several of his officers sat huddled over a map of Boston and the surrounding area. The fortifications occupied by the British blocked the narrow neck that connected Boston with the mainland. The positions occupied by the Continental forces all around the harbor were marked. The map made it clear: The military situation at Boston was at a stalemate.

Just after Lexington and Concord, in April 1775, the Continental militia had come swarming to the call to arms, and the British forces commanded by General Gage had been trapped. Once, in June, the Redcoats had made a sally, capturing the strategic position of Bunker Hill. They had paid such a price in blood for that effort, however, that no subsequent attacks had been made on Continental lines. That had been the case ever since George Washington had arrived to take command of the colonial forces.

But if the British could not get out of Boston, the Continentals could not get in. There were fantastic proposals being made about building a giant magnifying glass that would concentrate the sun's rays on houses in Boston and set them on fire, or floating barrels of gunpowder down the river with fuses set to explode the powder as they bobbed among the British ships. While the dreamers dreamed and the schemers schemed, the military men huddled. They knew something had to be done soon. The enlistments of most of the men in the Continental force were set to expire at the end of the year. Unless something was done to break the stalemate, it would be difficult to rouse the enthusiasm necessary to cause the veterans to reenlist and to recruit new men.

There was a reliable, effective way to get the British out of Boston: artillery—big guns. The Continentals had such weapons, but, unfortunately, they were 300 miles away at Fort Ticonderoga on Lake Champlain, over mountains and across the Hudson River. The distance and terrain meant the artillery might just as well have been on the moon. Or so thought most. Henry Knox wasn't so sure.

Henry Knox had little practical military experience, but he had read a lot. Before the war began, he had owned The London Book Store in Boston. Knox had made the store a haven for British officers stationed in the town and had kept a large stock of military titles, all of which he read himself and discussed with the officers. When war broke out, Knox abandoned his books and slipped out of town with his wife, herself the daughter of a British official. Now, Knox was ready to offer a suggestion that might break the stalemate around Boston.

Henry Knox offered to go to Fort Ticonderoga and select the guns to be brought to Boston. He would dismantle them and move them as far as he could by water. Then, he would build large sleds and wait for the snows to come. The surface of the snow would provide a smooth highway across the wilderness all the way to Boston. Having no better offer on hand, George Washington accepted Knox's proposal, and in November 1775, Henry Knox left for the frontier. Washington urged Knox to hurry with the big guns. "The want of them is so great that no Trouble or Expence must be spared to obtain them."

The trip to Ticonderoga was accomplished in about two weeks. Knox arrived on December 5. In only four days he had selected fifty-nine cannons and mortars, moved them overland a few miles to Lake George, and loaded them aboard a large scow. Several of the cannons Knox had chosen were large pieces that could fire twenty-four-pound balls at enemy fortifications. These guns weighed up to two thousand pounds each when mounted on their gun carriages. The mortars were huge, squat pieces of ordnance, some of which fired shells thirteen inches in diameter. The largest gun Knox selected weighed 5,500 pounds. Traveling by water was the easiest method of transporting goods on the frontier, but bad luck soon struck. Just off Sabbath Day Point, the scow was swamped by the waves and sank. The only good luck was that the water was shallow; somehow the boat and cargo were refloated. Knox did not leave an account as to how this was done, so historians are left with only imagination to supply the details. We do know that ordinary Americans of that day were accustomed to moving heavy weights primarily by muscle power. Levers, rollers, and block and tackle were familiar to the people of that time.

On December 17 the cannons had reached Fort George and were loaded aboard sleds pulled by 248 horses and 300 men. The ground was already covered with snow, providing a smooth surface for travel, where only rocks and rough ground existed in the summer. On Christmas Day a terrific snowstorm struck, and the drifts became too deep to travel through. However, on New Year's Eve the strange procession was again underway.

While crossing the Hudson River near Albany, disaster struck again. The ice broke under the weight of one of the largest of the cannons, and it sank from sight beneath the frigid surface of the water. Somehow, amid the snow, ice, and freezing water, volunteers managed to get ropes around the gun and, after two days of heaving, hauled it to the surface. Moving the gun to a place where the ice was still solid, Knox ordered holes cut through the ice so that water would come up from below, spread over the existing ice, and freeze, thus making the ice thicker. In honor of the assistance provided by the local citizens, the gun was named The Albany.

Once the Post Road was reached at Greenwich, the way appeared to be easier, but it wasn't. Ahead rose the Berkshire Mountains. Going up the west side was slow, but going down the eastern slopes was too fast. With no brakes to slow them, the sleds constantly threatened to run over the men and horses pulling them. Often, ropes had to be wrapped around trees to slow the descent, while other men, at the immanent risk of smashed hands and feet, had to jam poles under the skids on the sleds to retard their speed. A halt was made at Westfield because of a thaw. In exchange for whiskey and cider, Knox entertained the residents by firing off a large gun called The Old Sow. A return of cold weather ended the Westfield festivities. Assisted by eighty yoke of oxen, the guns reached Boston in late February.

On the night of March 3, 1776, the Continental Army put on a great show, pretending to prepare an attack on the British lines. While attention was focused on the north and west sides of Boston, Washington had 1,200 of his men haul the cannons to Dorchester Heights and build fortifications for them. The next morning the British army was literally staring down the barrels of the cannons from Ticonderoga.

Because the cannons could easily sink the ships in the harbor, their only hope of escape, the British troops immediately began to load their supplies aboard those ships and to leave Boston. Henry Knox would not have the satisfaction of saying his guns had blasted the British out of Boston, but he could say a good snow had convinced them to leave.

The Lowly Palmetto Defeats the Royal Oak

Two lines of one of the most popular songs sung by men of the Royal Navy during the eighteenth century were "Hearts of Oak are our ships. Jolly Tars are our men." Indeed, English oak was widely known among shipbuilders and sailors as the best wood in the world for warships. Tough and long lasting, the wood was so desirable that trees still standing in the forest were often blazed with the mark of the Broad Arrow making them "Royal Oaks," the property of the king.

Along the Carolina coast stood large numbers of another kind of tree, the palmetto. Most settlers treated it more as a weed than a tree. Its wood was soft and spongy, unfit for fires and impossible to saw into planks. Structures built of palmetto logs simply rotted away in three or four years. No one had a kind word to say for the palmetto tree, yet the lowly palmetto was destined to defeat the Royal oak.

The year 1776 would prove to be a roller-coaster year for Americans. The British evacuated Boston, and the thirteen colonies declared independence, forming a national government. But independence had to be made a reality, and the British were not going to allow that to happen easily.

As the citizens of America tried to make their independence more than just words on paper, the British sent a military expedition of ten warships and thirty transports, loaded with

2,000 men, to the southern colonies. Originally, the expedition planned to reinforce a group of Loyalist Americans in North Carolina, but this group was defeated and dispersed in a battle at Moores Creek Bridge. Gen. Henry Clinton and Adm. Sir Peter Parker then chose Charleston, South Carolina, as their alternative target.

In South Carolina great excitement spread with the word that the Crown's forces were coming. Many people in the colony had not yet decided which side to support in the war, but they were certain they would defend their homes. Soon, two regiments of troops had been raised, and their rosters read like a Who's Who of South Carolina society. The colonels of the regiments were Christopher Gadsden and William Moultrie. Other officers included Charles Cotesworth Pinckney and Francis Marion. These units were not a part of the Continental Line, the regular American army; instead they were South Carolina troops under the orders of the governor of that state.

Time was short, so defenses had to be constructed in a hurry. Colonel Moultrie was in command on Sullivan Island. He ordered two cribwork fences of palmetto logs to be built 10 feet high and 16 feet apart. The space between these two fences was then to be filled with sand. Both palmettos and sand were readily available on the island. Atop the palmetto-and-sand walls, twenty-five cannons were mounted, protected by yet more sand-and-palmetto barricades.

On the morning of June 8, 1776, the British fleet, led by the fifty-gun *Bristol* and the fifty-two-gun *Experiment*, sailed over the bar into Charleston Harbor. Fort Moultrie, as the sand-and-palmetto fortification was called, was far from finished. The fort was designed to be a square, with bastions projecting from each corner, but not a single wall of the fort was complete. For some reason the British fleet and accompanying troops did nothing for the next three weeks, while every day South Carolina axes felled palmettos and shovels made the sand fly.

On June 21 Gen. Charles Lee of the Continental Army came to inspect the fort and the state forces who had gathered to defend it. Lee was a professional soldier who had served in the British army, and he had little use for amateurs. After a brief look around the still unfinished fortification, Lee told Colonel Moultrie that it would only take a half hour of bombardment to make the fort nothing but a pile of matchsticks and sand, which would serve as a grave for any troops in it. Colonel Moultrie replied, "Then, Sir, the survivors will hide behind the ruins and whip the British anyway." On June 28 Moultrie got his chance to make good on these words.

On the morning of June 28, as soon as the tide was right, seven of the largest British ships sailed into line 400 yards from the fort. A smaller ship, *Thunder*, armed with fifteen-inch mortars, opened fire from 1½ miles away. The huge shells from this "bomb vessel" came whistling down and promptly buried themselves many feet deep in the marshy soil. Cannons from the warships began to fire as well, and soon seventy cannons were assaulting the fort. Moultrie fired back slowly and deliberately, and soon the British navy found it had a formidable opponent.

American cannonballs struck the hulls of the British ships, sending jagged splinters 3 and 4 feet long flying among the crowded crews. Other balls raked the British decks side to side or bow to stern. Sails were ripped to shreds and masts were cut off so that ships lost control and ran aground.

The British fire, however, hit the spongy palmetto logs and simply disappeared through them and into the tons and tons of sand piled behind the logs. The only visible damage the British accomplished was to shoot down the flagpole inside the fort. Because the troops in the fort were under the command of state authority, the flag on the pole was not the recently adopted Stars and Stripes of the young nation, but a blue banner bearing a silver crescent, a symbol long associated with South Carolina. On seeing the flag fall when the pole was shot in two, Sgt. William Jasper cut the flag loose from its rope halyards, tied it to a staff used to ram powder down the barrel of a cannon, and jabbed his makeshift flagpole into the sand of the fort wall.

In a last flurry of shots, the British flagship *Bristol* was heavily damaged, and the officer commanding the fleet, Adm. Sir Peter Parker, literally had his pants shot off. That was enough, he decided. The surviving British ships sailed away, leaving one of their number hard aground and burning. Almost one hundred British soldiers had been killed and more than three hundred were wounded. Thirty-seven South Carolina men were killed or wounded. It would be four years before the British returned to Charleston.

Today, the state seal of South Carolina shows a mighty oak lying in front of an erect palmetto, and the crescent on the state flag has been joined by a depiction of the lowly tree. In South Carolina it is still remembered that the lowly palmetto once defeated the Royal oak.

The Reluctant Author

He really did not want to be in Philadelphia that summer. It was hot, and he yearned for his cooler mountaintop. He was surrounded by people, but he liked solitude. Most of all, his wife was sick, and he felt the need to be with her.

Thomas Jefferson was not happy in his role as a delegate to the Second Continental Congress. He had actually left the assembly, with its interminable meetings and droning speakers, to go home to Virginia at the end of December 1775. His mother had been ill, and he had stayed at home to help care for her. His care was of no avail, for she died in March. Jefferson simply did not feel able to return to the Congress, and he consoled himself being busy with the affairs of his beloved Monticello and in nursing his wife, who had been ill for some time.

Finally, in mid-May, Jefferson bowed to the inescapable fact that he was an elected delegate to the Congress and returned to Philadelphia. That trip led to perhaps the most dramatic moment of his life, but he always wished he were elsewhere.

Truly, what was happening in Philadelphia did not seem nearly as significant as the events transpiring in Richmond. The assembly in Philadelphia was essentially a protest meeting. The delegates had no legal power; they were not members of a government, for no national government existed in America other than that of the King of England. They could not pass laws, levy taxes, or do much of anything. But in Richmond, as in many state capitals, constitutions were being written as the basis for new state governments. In these new state governments, both houses of the legislature and the governors would be elected. It was in these assemblies that the future was being forged, and Jefferson wanted to be a part of that process. Like any man of ability with even a shred of ambition, Jefferson wanted to be where the action was taking place.

Perhaps Jefferson even wished he had kept quiet back in 1774. At that time he had been a member of the Virginia House of Burgesses, and when the members of the First Continental Congress were elected, he was moved to write *A Summary View of the Rights of British America*. This pamphlet was a brash attack on not just the British government, but on King George III himself. Jefferson took the monarch to task for a variety of failings and ended by advising the king to be more honest if he wanted more sympathy from his people. That pamphlet's popularity had led to Jefferson's election as a delegate to the Second Continental Congress. But now he wanted to go home.

The mood of the Congress was shifting, slowly, toward separation from Britain. Six months earlier the bombshell of Thomas Paine's pamphlet *Common Sense* had exploded in the minds of Americans. Now that the path toward independence had been identified, it remained to be seen who would tread on it. On June 7, 1776, that question began to be answered when Richard Henry Lee, another Virginia delegate, proposed a resolution declaring that "these United Colonies are, and of right ought to be, free and independent states."

While Lee's resolution was being debated on the floor of Congress, those favoring independence succeeded in getting a committee appointed to prepare a formal declaration of independence, should Lee's motion pass. The members of the committee were Roger Sherman, Robert Livingston, John Adams, Benjamin Franklin, and Thomas Jefferson. Being a member of the committee left Jefferson with mixed opinions. He was afraid that the group might get bogged down in endless wrangling over the language and details of the declaration, but, on the other hand, at least something was being done that might lead to a conclusion of business.

At any rate it did not seem likely that Jefferson would be called on to do a lot of the work; he was the youngest and least-experienced member of the group. Franklin was a man of international renown as a writer and scientist; Adams was widely respected as a politician and statesman. Indeed, if Jefferson's old law professor, George Wythe, had been in town, the committee assignment probably would have gone to him, but Wythe had returned to Virginia to take care of personal business. So Jefferson was on the committee to write the declaration. But he wanted to go home.

As often happens, being the junior member of a committee meant that the work got dumped in his lap. Neither Franklin nor Adams showed much interest in being the author of the declaration, in part because no one thought it would become a famous, historic document. Franklin tended a little toward laziness, and Adams was much more interested in hatching political schemes with other delegates. Jefferson was a good writer. So Jefferson took the job of writing the declaration. Finish it, he thought, and go home.

Jefferson wrote a lot. He kept up a large correspondence about his plantation at Monticello, wrote daily to his wife, and frequently corresponded with his political friends back in Virginia. Too, there was considerable writing connected with the work of the Congress: reports, speeches, and such. To help him get through this work, Jefferson traveled with a writing box, a portable desk light enough to hold on his knees. It was five in the morning when Jefferson entered his parlor and went to work. The early rising habits of a country farmer had not deserted him. Besides, when he finished, he could go home. At nine o'clock he stood up to go to the statehouse where Congress was meeting.

The material Jefferson had written was good. He knew that. He had drawn on the classics and on common sense to lay out his ideas. Of great use was the list of American rights recently drawn up by George Mason, his fellow Virginian. What Jefferson dreaded was the debate.

The Congress had as members a number of men fond of the sound of their own voices and a number of others who felt they had to speak for the record on every issue. Jefferson was essentially a shy man, not given to public speaking. Fortunately, committee members John Adams and Benjamin Franklin could talk enough for all the members. And their talents were needed. After Lee's motion to declare independence had been taken up, the attention of Congress focused on the formal declaration prepared by Jefferson. For three interminable days words flew back and forth across the room. Jefferson suffered in silence as changes were suggested to his document. Some of them seemed like mutilations to his own flesh, but he kept quiet, hoping for an end to the debate.

Suddenly, it was over. In the evening of July 4, the room fell silent. Relatively few changes had actually been made, and they had only strengthened it. A "handsome copy" was ordered to be prepared for the delegates to sign, and the Declaration of Independence was read aloud to a cheering crowd on July 8. Before the end of the month, Jefferson was on his way home, never to serve in Congress again. He had been a reluctant author, but he had written one of the greatest documents in the history of government.

The Patriotic Political Parson

The horses of three men splashed through the pouring rain of a summer thunderstorm. The men on the horses were weary, having ridden almost 50 miles that day, and their sodden clothes were uncomfortable, but they had no thought of stopping short of Philadelphia. The three were delegates to the Continental Congress. At the meeting in Philadelphia, in this the second summer of the conflict with Great Britain, momentous decisions were being made. Independence was being discussed.

Ever since shots had been fired at Lexington and Concord on April 19, 1775, people had been trying to make a decision about the future of America. Was that future to be as colonies of a foreign power or as a sovereign people? The acknowledged leader of the three horsemen, John Witherspoon, had some pronounced ideas, and their clear articulation would soon move the Continental Congress toward the choice of independence.

The story is told that when King George III was presented with a copy of the Declaration of Independence, he read it through and then threw it to the floor shouting, "This is a damned Presbyterian plot." Even if the story is not completely true, the king's analysis of the document is accurate. John Witherspoon, one of the leading Presbyterian ministers in the American colony, helped to see to that. The teachings of the Presbyterian Church rest on a foundation provided by the

Protestant reformer John Calvin. It was Calvin's belief that only God should govern the consciences of people; all human government should begin with authority delegated to it by its citizens. (The Declaration of Independence would include this idea by stating that the government of this nation derives its just authority from the consent of the governed.) Calvin could not put his ideas into operation in the state in his lifetime, but he did make government by the people the basis for government in the church. Calvin's ideas had been brought to Scotland in the seventeenth century by John Knox. These ideas merged with the stubborn spirit of independence of the Scots. They also spread south, becoming the basis of the beliefs of the English Puritans and contributing to their civil war against King Charles I in the 1640s. With such an intellectual background, it is no wonder that John Witherspoon would favor independence.

Born in Scotland in 1722, the son of a Church of Scotland (Presbyterian) pastor, John Witherspoon entered the ministry himself at age twenty-one and began serving in the parish of Beith in 1745. Witherspoon opposed Charles Stuart when the "Young Pretender" came to Scotland from France in an attempt to begin a rebellion that would restore the Stuarts to the British throne. Witherspoon was not lacking in Scottish patriotism or in a belief in local rule, but he saw no need to replace one arbitrary monarch with another. Temporarily falling into the hands of Stuart supporters, the parson spent a brief time in prison before the collapse of the rebellion.

True to his principles of opposing arbitrary power and upholding local authority, Witherspoon stood against the leadership of the Church of Scotland when they tried to insist that ministers should be assigned to congregations instead of being chosen by the local church. His popularity as a speaker, preacher, and writer grew steadily, and Witherspoon became pastor of the large, prosperous church in Paisley in 1757. From there his reputation spread to America, where many Presbyterians worked to recruit Witherspoon as president of the

College of New Jersey, now known as Princeton. Those appeals were persuasive, and the Witherspoon family arrived in America in 1768.

The events leading up to the American Revolution were reaching a fever pitch as the decade of the 1760s drew to a close, and the new college president soon found himself associating with the leaders of the independence movement. At the commencement ceremonies of 1769, John Hancock was chosen to give the graduation address, while honorary degrees were awarded to John Dickinson and James Galloway, soon to be well-known revolutionary leaders. Among the students attracted to Princeton by the atmosphere Witherspoon created at the college were James Madison, principal writer of the Constitution and future president, and Henry Lee, later known as "Light Horse Harry" Lee, the leader of the Continental cavalry. (He would also become the father of the Civil War general Robert E. Lee.) In 1770, when the Boston Massacre occurred, Princeton students made a public demonstration of sympathy with the citizens of Boston. Witherspoon did not join in the demonstration, but neither did he oppose it. After the Boston Tea Party in 1773, Princeton students marched on the college dining hall and burned the supply of tea that had been purchased by the college steward. Again, Witherspoon did not attempt to stop or to punish the participants in the protest.

Witherspoon's reputation as a champion of American freedom spread, and he was made a member of the Committee of Correspondence of Somerset County, New Jersey. There were committees such as this in every county in each colony with the responsibility of keeping in touch with developments in the revolutionary movement in all areas of the country. These committees were the nerve endings of the revolution, moving local groups to action. On June 22, 1776, Witherspoon was elected a delegate to the Continental Congress in Philadelphia. So he went splashing through the mud and rain to take his seat.

The day after his soggy arrival, wearing dry clothes, John Witherspoon found himself lobbied by two competing factions in the Continental Congress. A liberal group wanted to declare independence at once, while a conservative party wanted to delay. Using the arrival of the fresh delegates from New Jersey as an excuse, the conservatives suggested that the debate over independence be reviewed for the benefit of the newcomers. Witherspoon wanted no delay. He declared, "The country is not only ripe for action, it is well nigh rotten for lack of it." That speech marked the end of delaying tactics. A few days later Witherspoon proudly stepped forward to affix his signature to the Declaration of Independence, the only clergyman to sign the document.

By the end of 1776, John Witherspoon and his family were refugees; the college of which he was president was closed, with most of its students enrolled in the Continental Army. One of the Witherspoon sons would lose his life in combat before the end of the war. Yet, John Witherspoon never looked back. He continued to serve in the Continental Congress until 1782. During his congressional career he served on more than one hundred committees, helped draft the Articles of Confederation, and assisted in writing the instructions to the American commissioners at the peace negotiations in Paris. Then he returned to Princeton for the rest of his life, working to build up the college he loved. He was truly a patriotic political parson.

A Little-Known Signer

"Gentlemen, when I give the word you may turn and fire when you are ready. Gentlemen, now!"

At the signal Lachlan McIntosh and Button Gwinnett turned to face one another. Separated by 20 yards, the traditional "pistol shot" of dueling lore, each man sighted down the barrel of his pistol, and then each squeezed the trigger. An instant later both fell to the ground. McIntosh was only lightly wounded, but Gwinnett had been struck in the body. Three days later, on May 19, 1777, Button Gwinnett died, having survived placing his name on the Declaration of Independence by less than one year.

What had caused these two men, both active patriots, to meet each other in murderous combat when their services were needed on the larger scene?

Button Gwinnett was born in Gloucester, England, in April 1735. The son of a Welsh clergyman, he married Ann Bourne in 1752, at which time he was a junior member of a firm trading with the American colonies. Hoping to improve their financial situation, Button and Ann came to the colonies. Settling first in Charleston, South Carolina, the couple soon moved to Savannah, Georgia, hoping for the financial success that always seemed to elude them.

In 1768 Gwinnett purchased 36 square miles of land on St. Catherine's Island off the Georgia coast and tried to become a successful planter. The plantation produced more frustration and debts than anything else, and financial ruin was always only a small step away.

Already feelings between the colonies and Britain were beginning to run high as the British Parliament tried to impose taxes on the colonies. Men who were in debt, such as Gwinnett, especially resented these added expenses. Not surprisingly, Gwinnett soon became a leading member of the Sons of Liberty. This group had been organized in 1765 to enforce a boycott of British goods in protest of the Stamp Act. Their actions were sometimes violent, but they proved effective in keeping British goods off the market. Although the organization in the South was not as radical as it was around Boston, the Sons of Liberty successfully blocked the importation of tea into Savannah when the British attempted to put a heavy tax on tea.

It was just at this time, however, that Gwinnett had severe financial troubles. He sold most of his property in an attempt to pay his debts and disappeared from public life.

The beginning of the war called Gwinnett back into the fray, and his neighbors elected him to command the Georgia troops serving in the Continental Army, which was beginning to assemble at Boston. Unfortunately, Gwinnett had made numerous enemies around the state in his financial dealings, and he had to resign in order for the state to raise a sufficient number of men for the Continental unit. As a compromise he was made the Georgia delegate to the Continental Congress, and Lachlan McIntosh got the military post.

Gwinnett arrived in Philadelphia on May 20, 1776. There is no record of his making speeches, but he served on various committees, and when the vote was taken to separate from Britain, he voted "Aye." Two days later, on July 4, he signed the Declaration of Independence.

Like many of the other delegates, including Thomas Jefferson, Gwinnett was anxious to get back to his home state where the real political action was taking place. By early autumn Gwinnett was back in Georgia and became Speaker of the Assembly. In this office he was a key figure in writing the original state constitution for Georgia.

When the state legislature adjourned, Gwinnett was named chairman of the Council of Safety, a position that made him commander of the state militia. At last the military command he desired was his. Perhaps he could win martial glory and that, in turn, would bring financial success.

Not far from Savannah was the Spanish territory of Florida. Although there was no quarrel between the fledgling United States and Spain, the British had already moved into West Florida, and it was feared that all Florida would fall into the hands of Britain. This feeling became especially strong after Britain and Spain went to war, although Spain did not become an ally of the United States. It was thought to be a good idea for Georgia forces to take control of Florida before Britain could move. As commander of the Georgia militia, Gwinnett prepared to march south.

From the first there were problems. Lachlan McIntosh, commander of the Continental troops in Georgia, refused to cooperate in what he labeled an ill-considered, poorly planned scheme. Convinced there was more than personal ill will behind McIntosh's refusal to help, Gwinnett went looking for traitors. Gwinnett decided he had found one in McIntosh's brother, and soon the young man was in prison. Clearly, McIntosh and Gwinnett were moving toward a confrontation which, in those days, legally allowed them to use deadly force.

The expedition into Florida was a predictable failure. Public opinion in Georgia turned against Gwinnett so strongly that he lost the election for governor, held under the new constitution that he had helped write. The Georgia legislature investigated the Florida invasion and ruled Gwinnett had done no wrong in his conduct of the affair.

McIntosh took the legislative finding as an implied criticism of his actions. If Gwinnett had done no wrong, then the implication was that McIntosh had. At a gathering of the social and political elite, General McIntosh publicly said Gwinnett was "a Scroundrell and lying Rascal," words he knew would bring both men to the dueling ground.

By the time the duel took place, Gwinnett was completely destitute. His St. Catherine's property had been raided by the Royal Navy, and everything he owned had been destroyed. When he died three days after the duel, the people who buried him had so little concern for him that they failed to mark his grave or even to leave a record of its location. There is no reliable portrait of him, and no modern biography of the man has been written.

The men who signed the Declaration of Independence pledged their "lives, fortunes, and sacred honor." Button Gwinnett lost two of the three within a year of putting his signature on the document. Little known, he still lies in an unmarked grave.

Author's note: Button Gwinnett was not the only member of the Continental Congress to suffer loss as a result of signing the Declaration. Francis Hopkinson had his home looted by the Hessians within a year of the signing. Richard Stockton's house became the headquarters for the Royal Army during the Battle of Princeton in January 1777. One of his own relatives told the British where Stockton was hiding, and he was arrested. Imprisoned under extremely harsh conditions, Stockton eventually agreed to sign a pledge to "remain in peaceful obedience to his Majesty." John Witherspoon had his house looted and his personal library burned. John Hart was, by the standards of the day, an old man of sixty-five when he signed. Within the next year there was such a fierce manhunt for Hart that he did not dare spend more than a single night in the same place.

Another Midnight Ride

Listen, my children, and you shall hear,
Of the midnight ride of Paul Revere . . .

These words by Henry Wadsworth Longfellow fixed the fame of the man who rode out from Boston on the night of April 18–19, 1775, to spread the alarm that the Royal Army was on the march against the Patriots. But Paul Revere was not the only messenger who ever rode through the night to rouse the countryside, nor was his trip the longest or most dangerous. That honor should go to Betsy Dowdy, a sixteen-year-old resident of the Outer Banks of North Carolina.

As the fever of war began to spread across the colonies following April 19, no place was left untouched. In every colony the Royal governors, men appointed to their posts by the king and not answerable to the people they governed, found it advisable to seek refuge wherever they could. In Virginia, Governor Dunmore collected a few British regulars from scattered army garrisons, abandoned the capital at Williamsburg, and began raising havoc at Suffolk and other places near the Virginia coast not far from the border with North Carolina. Governor Tryon of North Carolina went aboard the Royal Navy vessel *Cruzier* and began to rally Loyalist sentiment along the coast, especially among the Scots who were recent immigrants from Britain. Both governors tried to convince slaves to rally to the Royal cause, promising them freedom in exchange for fighting. Caught between these growing British forces, the residents along the North Carolina coast and on the Outer Banks were especially vulnerable to attack.

As George Washington and his army laid siege to the British in Boston, Patriots in Virginia and North Carolina rallied to meet the threat against them. A vital strategic point was the Great Bridge across the Elizabeth River, presently the location of the town of Chesapeake, Virginia. This river crossing was a key location on the only decent road leading from the Norfolk area south into Carolina. If the British controlled the bridge, the North Carolina coast would be open to invasion; if the Patriots held the bridge, the British could be driven away from the important port of Norfolk. The British had constructed a fort at the north end of the bridge. Because the soil was marshy, the fort was built entirely of wood and was not especially strong, but it kept the bridge available for British use while denying it to the Patriots.

By late November 1775 militia from Virginia were moving toward the contested area, but more Patriot militiamen were needed. The best man to rally and lead the needed troops was Gen. William Skinner of North Carolina, who lived on Yeopin Creek. There was some question, however, as to whether or not General Skinner knew just how badly the North Carolina militia were needed at Great Bridge.

Early in December Sammy Jarvis, a resident of the Outer Banks who lived near Knotts Island, crossed to the mainland in search of news about developing events. What he heard about the depredations being committed among the Virginia Patriots by Governor Dunmore and his men caused him a great deal of alarm, and he returned to the Outer Banks to spread the warning. In due course Jarvis reached the residence of Joseph Dowdy on Currituck Island. Arriving late in the day, Jarvis was invited to spend the night and share all his news. Dowdy earned his living by fishing and by salvaging goods from wrecked ships. In addition he caught, trained, and sold the famous Banks ponies, wild horses said to be descended from equine survivors of ships wrecked along the beaches of the Outer Banks. Dowdy had a herd of several hundred Banks ponies, and he knew that his horses would be high on the list of goods the British forces would want to take for their own use. Dowdy became quite apprehensive about the danger to his home and goods, agreeing that General Skinner ought to be alerted and roused to go fight.

Listening to the conversation between the men was Betsy Dowdy, the sixteen-year-old daughter of the household. When Jarvis jokingly asked what she would do if the British came to take her favorite horse, Black Bess, the young woman replied that she would hit them over the head with a conch shell. But as the conversation grew more serious, Betsy quietly left the room. Without saying a word to either of her parents, Betsy went outside and called to her horse. Placing only a blanket on the back of Black Bess, she mounted and rode away into the gathering winter darkness. The danger in this situation should not be underestimated. For a sixteen-year-old on such a trip in such terrain, drowning was a very real possibility, as was attack by a wild animal. In the sparsely settled countryside, there would be no light showing in any cabin she might pass, no help in any emergency. But Betsy felt the warning had to be delivered.

Like any person living near the sea, Betsy was keenly aware of the tides, and she knew the tide was out at that hour. This meant the water between the various islands was shallow enough for her horse to cross without swimming, if the rider knew the lay of the land. Betsy did. She also knew the shortest route to reach the mainland. Riding across Currituck, she splashed over to Church's Island, across a broader expanse of water to Camden, then to Lamb's Ferry. At Lamb's she had to cross a deep channel, and there was no choice but for horse and rider to swim. For the rest of the trip in the sharp night air,

Betsy would be soaking wet. Through Pasquotank to Hartsford and on to Perquimans, the black horse carried the shivering girl. As the sun rose, Betsy Dowdy and Black Bess reached General Skinner's house on Yeopin Creek, 50 miles from their starting place on Currituck Island.

In the face of this feat of courage and daring, General Skinner could not doubt the seriousness of the situation, and a call was immediately sent out to the North Carolina militia to march for the Great Bridge. But Betsy did not stay long to rest. She also heard the call to duty, the duty to return home and attend to her chores. After taking a meal, Betsy and her remarkable horse started the long ride back to Currituck.

On December 9, 1775, Governor Dunmore decided to attack before the North Carolina reinforcements could arrive. The British force crossed the Great Bridge and attacked over a narrow causeway. The attackers never had a chance against the Patriot riflemen. Only a few North Carolina militiamen had arrived in time to participate in the battle, but more came into the Patriot camp over the next several days. Even if the men were late, Betsy Dowdy had done her part well. Her midnight ride is still an amazing example of fortitude and courage.

Blue Coat or Red?

Which side should he support? This was the issue facing every one of the Africans living in the colonies as the Revolutionary War began. Although English and European settlers might argue over carefully defined issues such as the right to tax, the colonists of African descent faced a much simpler question. Who would make them free? Should they put on the blue coat of the Continental Army or the red coat of the Royal Army? Who was offering the best deal? The answer would not be simple or clear. Slavery was legal in all British colonies, though not in Britain itself. Would Britain really set a slave free in a colony where the law upheld the institution? Would Britain encourage the growth of a class of freed slaves in the midst of a slave-holding society? What were the African colonists to do?

No census was taken in colonial America at regular intervals, but the usually accepted estimate is that some 2.5 million people lived in the American colonies at the outbreak of the Revolution. Of this number about 20 percent, or 500,000 people, were of African descent. Most of these were slaves. These people were not spread evenly throughout the colonies. In New England about 3 percent of the population was Black, while farther south the number rose to 33 percent. In Georgia Blacks outnumbered Whites. The larger their number, relative to the total population, the more strictly the slaves were controlled and the fewer were the opportunities offered to free people of color. These factors affected the participation of African colonists in the war and helped dictate the side they chose to support.

When the war began, free men of color were among the first soldiers. In the reports filed by the Minutemen concerning the fighting at Lexington on April 19, 1775, the first real battle of the war, there is the note "wounded—Prince Easterbrooks, Negro." Also recorded as fighting on that day with the Minutemen was Peter Salem, a free African American. A few weeks later Peter Salem and Salem Poor, both men of color, were on duty with the Patriots on Bunker Hill. Poor so distinguished himself that he was given a certificate of commendation signed by fourteen officers.

Throughout the colonies, enslaved Africans were taken to war by their masters who wanted help with the work necessary to life in camp. On occasion these "servants," as they were always called, voluntarily went into combat. The most famous of these occasions is depicted in the well-known painting, *Battle of Cowpens*. In this battle scene Col. William Washington of the Continental cavalry is dueling with one British cavalryman and is about to be attacked with a saber by the British commander Banistre Tarleton. Preventing the attack from being pressed home is Washington's "servant," who is shown firing a pistol at Tarleton. The irony of this situation is that while memorialized in a well-known painting the name of the Black man is not known. William Washington never wrote anything about the incident.

Only a few months after the battle at Bunker Hill in June 1775, a policy was approved by the council of officers of the Patriot forces that excluded "all Negroes, slave as well as free" from the army. The free Africans in the army were quite upset by this policy and took their grievance to the army commander. After listening to their protest, George Washington agreed and overruled the policy of the council so these men could continue to serve their country.

As the war continued its slow course, events began to force army officers to reconsider their attitudes toward exclusion. One factor was the "natural rights" philosophy that underlay the Declaration of Independence. Having declared that "all men . . . are endowed by their creator with the right to life, liberty, and the pursuit of happiness," it became increasingly difficult to deny liberty to a large class of people. Another factor was the simple need for men. In several colonies white men wanted to send substitutes to fight for them. When no white substitutes could be found, they wanted to send black men. In Rhode Island the state government began purchasing slaves and granting them freedom upon enlistment in the Continental Army. The Rhode Island regiment would become well known after an engagement with the British in their home state. The Continental troops had advanced onto the island in Providence Bay expecting to be met by ships of their French allies. Instead, the Royal Navy showed up and began landing troops. The Continentals had to make a fighting withdrawal, and the difficult and dangerous post of rear guard was held by the Rhode Island regiment of one-time slaves. Their fighting spirit won the respect of both armies. Lastly, British actions exerted pressure. The Redcoats offered freedom to male slaves and their families if the men would come into the British lines and do any type of useful work for the armed forces. Thousands of African Americans accepted the offer.

Perhaps five thousand black men, slave and free, served in the Patriot forces, but four or five times that number aided the British. At the opening of the war, Lord Dunmore, Royal Governor of Virginia, offered to free any man who joined his Ethopian Regiment. Soon Dunmore had several hundred men under arms, and they participated in numerous raids and skirmishes in the Chesapeake Bay area. In the North the British army adopted the same idea. After the British occupation of New York City in 1776, that location became a magnet for slaves seeking freedom. For the rest of the war, the British commander in New York had all the labor force he needed, and sometimes there were more workers than work. In this circumstance the British began sending those African Americans who had been with the army the longest to Nova Scotia, where they were set free. An unknown number of ex-slaves were liberated in that way.

The best-known recruit to the British cause was a New Jersey slave named Ty. After gaining his freedom by joining the British, he became the leader of a band of scouts that made guerrilla attacks in Patriot territory. Not many records of his exploits were made, but it is clear Ty was a terror to the Patriots until he was killed in combat in September 1777.

When the British focused their military efforts in the South, beginning in 1779, they continued to recruit those who sought freedom. At Savannah and Charleston large numbers of former slaves joined the British. When the war ended in 1783, between fifteen and twenty thousand ex-slaves joined the retreating British on the road to freedom in other British colonies.

The Revolution's ideals of liberty and justice were just that—ideals. They would be realized only slowly and, for some, would be realized first under the Union Jack, not the Stars and Stripes. But the American nation had started down a road from which there would be no turning back.

Legendary Long Rifles

The British officer peered carefully across the clearing toward the woods more than 200 yards away. No enemy was in the field, so it was safe to start across. He and his patrol would be well out of musket range until they were more than halfway across the open ground. Stepping into the field the officer saw a puff of smoke spurt up from the far woodline. It was the last physical sensation he would ever experience. Before the "crack" of the shot could reach his ears, he fell dead with a .45-caliber rifle ball through his heart. The men in his patrol were understandably discouraged by this event and returned to their lines, carrying the body of their officer, but without completing their mission.

Many British officers fell victim to the legendary long rifle wielded by a Patriot frontiersman. Today, they are often called "Kentucky rifles," but during the Revolution they were known as "Pennsylvania rifles" or "long rifles." These weapons represented a technological revolution that would eventually transform the battlefield.

The firing mechanism on the rifle was the same as that used on muskets. The difference between a rifle barrel and a musket was inside the barrel. In a rifle were spiral grooves cut into the metal that caused the rifle ball to spin in its flight, thus attaining much greater accuracy and range than a musket ball. This technological development did not originate in America, but it became synonymous with the American frontier.

The rifle developed in the alpine region of Europe and was especially associated with the German huntsman or "Jaeger." German settlers brought their rifles with them to wildernesses of the New World. The Jaeger rifles were too short-barreled to develop high muzzle velocity and were too heavy to carry on hunts that might last weeks or months. Also, their large caliber used great quantities of powder and shot. All these characteristics were drawbacks on the frontier.

Out of conversations between frontiersmen and gunsmiths, there evolved the "long rifle." A longer barrel gave great muzzle velocity, which caused smaller bullets to hit harder. The small caliber saved powder and shot. To speed up loading while retaining the accuracy created by a tightly fitting bullet, the rifle ball was slightly smaller than the bore but was wrapped in a patch of greased cloth. The resulting weapon was accurate at a range that the eighteenth century considered extremely long, relatively light in weight, conservative in its consumption of powder and shot, and esthetically appealing in its graceful lines.

The most famous maker of long rifles was Jacob Dickert of Pennsylvania, but his ideas were copied by gunsmiths all up and down the frontier. The caliber of these weapons varied from .35 to .60, but .45 and .50 were the most popular sizes, with barrel lengths of 36 to 48 inches.

Militarily, rifles had some drawbacks. Unlike muskets, which could be manufactured relatively quickly and cheaply, rifles were individual creations of master gunsmiths who worked long hours with relatively crude tools to cut the rifling grooves into the barrels. The weapons also took a comparatively long time to load. An experienced musketman could get off four or five shots while a rifleman was firing and reloading once. In eighteenth-century warfare the volume of fire was more important than accuracy, so muskets ruled the battlefield and would for almost another century. Tactics would also continue to reflect the presence of a short-range infantry weapon with limited accuracy. Finally, rifles were primarily hunting weapons and were not made to receive a bayonet. The climactic moment of most eighteenth-century battles was a bayonet charge, so riflemen were of limited usefulness in such situations. In hand-to-hand fighting, the frontier rifleman used a knife or a tomahawk.

It was its range that made the long rifle a feared weapon. While accurate musket range was around 80 yards, a skilled rifleman could consistently hit targets at 300 yards, almost four times the effective range of a musket. This meant the person in the rifleman's sights would literally never know who or what hit them. The British considered such tactics as deliberately aimed fire at a specific target to be "ungentlemanly," but the frontier riflemen did not consider themselves gentlemen. They were, however, good shots.

The riflemen made their first appearance on the battlefield in late August 1775, when a company commanded by Daniel Morgan joined George Washington's army at the Siege of Boston. Dressed in a leather or linen hunting shirt that came halfway between his knees and thighs and was belted at the waist, the riflemen were effectively camouflaged. Breeches with leggings and moccasins completed the distinctive dress of the long-rifle-carrying frontiersman. This appearance alone astonished both the militia from the settled areas and the nattily uniformed British. For these men shooting was a serious matter, not a sport. Domestic meat animals were scarce on the frontier, and a family's food supply might well depend on one's accuracy with a rifle. In a more direct fashion, family security from danger depended on the family's firearms and the ability to use them well.

Before being sent out to snipe at the British, the riflemen gave a demonstration of what they and their rifles could do. The entire company consistently put ball after ball into a 17-inch-wide target at a range of 250 yards. At 150 yards some of the riflemen held the target between their knees while their comrades shot holes into it. These marksmen soon had made such an impression on the British that Washington gave orders that they should not fire unless they had a clear shot. He did not want misses to ruin their reputation.

After the British evacuation of Boston, the riflemen were sent north to join the Patriot army under Gen. Horatio Gates, who was guarding the Lake Champlain–Hudson River approach to New England. When fighting erupted at Freeman's Farm on September 19, 1777, Daniel Morgan's men found themselves opposing a force of one hundred men commanded by Maj. Gordon Forbes of the Royal Army. Within five minutes every officer in Forbes's force was dead or wounded. The riflemen looked for men with epaulets or silver gorgets and killed them first. During later fighting at Saratoga, one of the British division commanders, Simon Frasier, was deliberately targeted and killed by a sharp-eyed Patriot rifleman.

When the British retreated from Saratoga on October 10, 1777, their rear guard constructed a small redoubt with log walls 4 feet high. Knowing Morgan and his riflemen were coming after them, the British soldiers stayed flat on the ground behind the logs. Finally, a man lifted his cap on the ramrod of his musket. Three rifle balls hit the cap simultaneously.

Throughout the rest of the war, whenever circumstances favored small-scale skirmishing, the men with the long rifles found their niche. At Cowpens, Kings Mountain, and a dozen more battles, the men and their weapon carved themselves a place in the history of the emerging nation.

What Washington Really Said While Crossing the Delaware

The big man on the sorrel horse was disgusted and mad. He was disgusted with the weather, the clock, his subordinates, his army, his government, and himself. He was mad at the pretentious European officers who tried to stab him in the back, the cautious councils of war, being ridiculed by his enemies, and losing every battle he fought. Now he was going to strike back, even if he had to strike back alone.

The Revolution was about over to all appearances. The colonies had created a Continental Army on January 1, 1776, with a strength of more than twenty thousand men. A lanky, aristocratic fox-hunting farmer from Virginia named George Washington had been chosen its commander. The colonies had declared their independence on July 4 of the same year. Full of pride and confidence, the Continental Army had marched down to New York City to defend the town and had gotten caught in the meat grinder of the British army in action. The British had the most professional, best-trained army on the face of the planet. They not only knew the book on military operations, they had written it. When brought to battle in the open, without earthworks for protection, Washington's amateur soldiers never stood a chance. For some of these amateurs, death came suddenly and violently from British musket balls or bayonets. Others sought safety by running. The Continental Army soon proved to be very good at running. Day after day, mile after mile, they fell back, and for every hour spent in retreat, a soldier slipped away and went home.

All of them would be going home soon. The enlistments the men had signed on January 1, 1776, would expire on December 31. When that day came, Washington would have no army at all. At this time Washington wrote his brother, Augustine, "I think the game is pretty near up."

Finally, the Delaware River came into view. Washington sent out patrols to sweep up and down the river for miles. All boats were to be destroyed except for larger ones, which were to be saved for the army. Among these larger boats, Washington wanted saved some four dozen Durham boats, originally designed and built to haul pig iron to Philadelphia. The boats were double-ended and propelled by poling. They averaged 8 feet in width, 40 to 60 feet in length, and could carry up to fifteen tons while drawing only 30 inches of water. Empty, the boats drew only 5 inches. Once Washington was across the Delaware, he could hold off the British, at least until the river froze over. Before then he had to think of something.

As the remaining days of the soldiers' terms of enlistment trickled down to near zero, Washington managed to regroup all the men under his command. With some six thousand men under his control, Washington conceived a daring plan.

On the east side of the Delaware River, two units of German mercenaries had been assigned to hold the front line. These German troops were called Hessians, even though only a few of them came from the German state of Hesse. Col. Johann Rahl commanded a garrison of troops at Trenton, while Col. Count Carl von Donop commanded a garrison at Bordentown. Washington planned to lead a column of troops against

Trenton, aided by a secondary attack led by the Pennsylvania militia under Gen. James Ewing. Col. John Cadwalader would lead the troops garrisoning Philadelphia against Bordentown. Such a bold move might revive the spirits of both the army and the nation.

Gen. Horatio Gates was second in command of the Patriot forces. He pointed out that Washington was proposing to have three widely separated bodies of men, most of whom lacked proper training, experience, and discipline, cross a wide river choked with ice, and make a converging attack on a force of veteran professional soldiers. Gates judged such a course to be suicidal. Rather than support Washington, Gates reported himself sick and rode off to Philadelphia.

Washington had listened to advice from subordinates before, and he had become convinced that they were lacking in the determination necessary to win the war. On this occasion Washington was going to listen to himself.

Washington's resolve, and that of the army, was boosted by Thomas Paine, who published one of his most famous pamphlets just at the right moment. "These are the times that try men's souls. . . . " Paine wrote in *The Crisis*, "but he that stands it *now,* deserves the love and thanks of man and woman." By order of the general, the pamphlet was read aloud to each company at Evening Parade.

On Christmas Eve night, Washington called his officers together and revealed his plans. At dark on Christmas Day, the army would begin crossing the river in the Durham boats. The actual crossing would be handled by Col. John Glover and his unit of Massachusetts fishermen. After crossing the Delaware at McConkeys Ferry, the army would march 9 miles to attack Rahl at Trenton, breaking into two columns just outside the village to converge on the German encampment from two directions. Rotund artillery commander Henry Knox was pleased to hear eighteen of his beloved cannons would accompany the assault force.

As the officers left the meeting in the early hours of Christmas Day, they found snow falling and large cakes of ice swirling in the current of the river. Christmas Day was hardly a time of celebration in the Patriot ranks. There was little food, although the citizens of Philadelphia did send out a couple of wagons filled with old clothes to supplement their ragged uniforms. Throughout the daylight hours, the army assembled just short of McConkeys Ferry, hidden behind a low ridge, and the Durham boats assembled on the lee of an island. Darkness brought with it a freezing rain that began to soak the soldiers' clothing, making them even colder than the snow had. And, of course, the fading light increased the confusion as men began pouring over the hill and down to the stream.

A regiment of Virginia riflemen went first across the river to secure a beachhead; the rest of the army followed as fast as John Glover could stuff them into the Durham boats. In the darkness and confusion, it was obvious to all that the entire operation was falling behind schedule, the chance of surprising the Germans was slipping away, and morning might bring another disaster instead of a victory.

Washington sensed the mood of his men. He knew that many of them saw him as nothing but an aloof, fox-hunting Virginia aristocrat. He also knew that now was the time to replace that image with a more personal one. When the time came for Washington and his staff to cross the river, they climbed aboard a Durham boat already loaded with two cannons and twenty men. Making his way to an empty seat, Washington spoke loudly, so that the entire assembled force could hear him. His words were not historic, or even inspirational, but they struck just the right note to carry the army through the wet, freezing night and on to victory the next morning.

Turning to his chief of artillery, Washington said, "Hell, Henry, shift your fat butt, but be careful. You'll swamp this [expletive] boat."

The Posthumous Prisoner of War

The Patriot army was always in need of military supplies, and this was especially true in January 1777. Even so, one wagon of captured goods contained a powerful surprise.

The supply situation had improved some since December of the preceding year when Washington had led his tiny force across the icy Delaware River to attack the Hessians at Trenton. That victory had awakened some enthusiasm for the cause, and now Gen. George Washington had led his men across the river again.

To the British commander Lord Howe, it appeared Washington was merely revisiting the scene of his former victory, because the Patriot army was again in Trenton. Howe ordered Gen. Lord Cornwallis to move to Princeton, gather his troops, and advance on Trenton. On January 2, 1777, Cornwallis advanced with 6,000 men, leaving three regiments to guard his base at Princeton.

All day on January 2, the Patriot troops fought as they slowly fell back on Trenton. By nightfall the British were in the streets of the village facing the Patriot position.

Washington had moved to the south bank of Assunpink Creek and entrenched his men on a ridge. From the front the position looked strong, but its right flank was unguarded. Even worse, the Delaware River blocked any line of retreat. It looked to Cornwallis that Washington had made just the sort of mistake one would expect of an amateur. Washington's army was in a trap, and Cornwallis let it be known he was ready to bag the fox. The Patriot army was ready to fight from behind breastworks as they had done so well at Bunker Hill. Only this time the British would not oblige them by attacking head-on. Cornwallis planned to turn the unprotected flank and butcher the Patriots as they tried to flee across the Delaware River.

During the night, as Cornwallis fed and rested his men so they would be ready for the fox hunt the next morning, Washington's army slipped away by its undefended flank, moving toward Princeton. Daylight revealed the Royal Army confronting only empty entrenchments. The fox had run instead of going to ground.

As dawn broke on January 3, Col. Charles Mawhood of the Seventeenth Infantry was moving toward Trenton to join other parts of the British army. Left in Princeton were the Fortieth and Fifty-fourth Regiments. Moving toward Mawhood, each ignorant of the other's presence, was a Patriot unit led by Gen. Hugh Mercer. As the two units converged on the hill known today as Mercer Heights, gunfire began. Following their usual practice, the Patriot riflemen aimed for the British officers. Among the first to fall was Capt. William Leslie of the British Seventeenth Regiment.

William Leslie was a son of Lord Leven of Scotland and a nephew of Gen. Alexander Leslie. As a member of one of the most famous military families in Scotland, William joined the Black Watch Regiment as a teen and served with that unit in Ireland. In 1776 William got a promotion and joined the Seventeenth Infantry. He was well liked by his men and fellow officers and was described as being sweet-natured, compassionate, and kindly.

Falling a casualty to one of Mercer's long rifles, William's body was placed in a baggage wagon by a fellow officer. Unsure just how many men were facing him but confident in the ability of his men to handle the challenge, Mawhood pushed forward. At first the attack was a success because Mercer's command was composed of riflemen. Their weapons, though accurate at a longer range, were slower to load than muskets, and the rifles were not fitted with bayonets. Mercer was reinforced by Pennsylvania troops under Gen. John Cadwalader. Hand-to-hand fighting occurred before the Redcoat attack was blunted, and Mawhood fell back on the two regiments left in Princeton.

Washington was in the thick of the fight, sometimes within 30 yards of the British lines, inspiring his men by his example and by his cheering taunt of the British, "Come on. Bag the fox! How do you Lobsterbacks like this fox-hunt?" Later Washington would describe his emotions at the moment in a letter to a friend. "I have heard the musket balls sing about my ears and I tell you they make a delightful music." Capt. William Leslie would have disagreed had he been able to do so.

Some of the British barricaded themselves in Nassau Hall on the campus of Princeton University. Musket balls splatted harmlessly against the thick stones of the walls, but Henry Knox brought up two cannons and the last British holdouts soon surrendered.

Washington had won a neat victory over three crack British regiments, but he knew Lord Cornwallis, with 6,000 men, was moving against his rear as fast as they could cover the route back from Trenton. Gathering his booty, including British wagons, Washington marched to Pluckemin, where he was protected by the rugged terrain of the Watchung Mountains.

On January 5, 1777, the needy Patriot troops began to unload the captured wagons. With gleaming eyes and eager hands, they unpacked boxes of musket ammunition, crates of hardtack crackers, bales of warm overcoats, and sturdy boots. But in one wagon was a real surprise—a British officer, dead. William Leslie had become a prisoner of war, albeit a posthumous prisoner. Searching the body in an attempt to identify the officer, the soldiers found another surprise. In Leslie's pocket was a letter from Dr. Benjamin Rush, a leader of the independence movement.

Dr. Rush had studied medicine in Edinburgh and had met

the Leslie family while a student there. Indeed, he had fallen in love with Jean, William's sister. Jean did not wish to marry someone from the colonies, but the families remained good friends. When the war broke out, Dr. Rush had written to Captain Leslie to say that if the captain should ever be captured, Rush would guarantee his parole and would try to have him released to his custody, so he would not have to remain in a prison camp. The doctor now made good his promise in an unexpected way.

Out of respect to Dr. Rush, General Washington intervened in the matter of Captain Leslie and ordered the British officer buried with full military honors. After the war Dr. Rush located the grave and, at his own expense, erected a stone that bears the following epitaph:

In Memory of
The Honorable Capt Wm Leslie
of the 17th British Regiment
Son of the Earl of Leven
in Scotland
He fell Jany 3d 1777 Aged
26 years at the battle of
Princeton
His friend Benjn Rush M D of
Philadelphia
hath caused this stone
to be erected as a mark
of his esteem for his worth
and of his respect for his noble Family

Capt. William Leslie is the only British fatality of the Battle of Princeton to be buried in an individual grave. He is the only known posthumous prisoner of war in the entire Revolutionary War.

The Loyal Leg

The mere mention of Benedict Arnold's name is likely to be greeted by most American audiences with boos and hisses. His name has become a synonym for traitor, a man who betrayed his country in exchange for money and recognition. But it was not always so, and Arnold's long-ago loyalty has led to the creation of the strangest monument to be found on any American battlefield.

When the struggle for independence began, an observer would have been hard put to find a more enthusiastic patriot than Benedict Arnold. Thirty-six years old, about five feet, nine inches tall, Arnold was stocky and had about him an air of restless energy, very much like a panther. His cold gray eyes, jet black hair, and swarthy skin gave him a look some found sinister. But when danger arose and combat began, Arnold became an inspiring combat commander. He seemed to know just where his presence was needed on the field of battle, and his stamina and determination to let nothing stand in his way seemed to communicate themselves to troops under his command.

In the opening days of the war, Arnold had assisted Ethan Allen in the capture of Fort Ticonderoga on Lake Champlain. Following that, Arnold had been in command of troops under Richard Montgomery in an abortive invasion of Canada. In 1776, after being released as a prisoner of war, Arnold had helped to cobble together a fleet of small boats on Lake Champlain. He led these into battle near Valcour Island, and, although he lost the battle, he so badly damaged the British fleet that no farther advance was possible that year. In the fall of

1777, Arnold again was getting ready to go into action in the same area.

In August 1776 the British army and navy, in a combined operation, had captured New York City and had seriously damaged Washington's army. With the mouth of the Hudson River firmly in their hands, the British high command planned to push an army of British and hired German soldiers, commanded by Gen. John Burgoyne, down from Canada and along Lake Champlain. The force would capture Fort Ticonderoga, move on overland to the Hudson River, capture Albany, and link the forces in New York with those coming from Canada. This would sever New England from the other states and might well lead to the end of the war with a British victory. "Gentleman Johnny" Burgoyne was anxious for higher command and for civil honors, and he was supremely confident he could do this job, especially if the forces in New York City came to meet him.

To stop this plan, American hopes were pinned on an army commanded, at first, by Gen. Philip Schuyler and, later, by Gen. Horatio Gates, a man so cautious as to be called "Granny Gates." Arnold commanded a unit in this army, but he was all too well aware that men with less experience had been promoted over him. Perhaps this campaign would be his chance to regain prominence.

Although he made a start late in the season, General Burgoyne moved steadily along the chosen route south. Thousands of men and tons of supplies moved along Lake Champlain. The mere approach of Burgoyne's force caused the Americans to evacuate Fort Ticonderoga, a post they could not have defended successfully. The retreating Americans then took up a position on Bemis Heights near Saratoga, New York, where they could block both the crude road to Albany and the Hudson River.

General Burgoyne was depending for help on an expedition coming down the Mohawk River, an army of Canadians and Indians that would capture the American-held Fort Stanwix before uniting with Burgoyne. Arnold was given the duty of making sure Fort Stanwix stayed in American hands.

As Arnold marched toward the surrounded fort, his cunning came to the fore. Arnold recruited a mentally challenged man named Hon Yost, who was believed to have supernatural powers because he spoke in "unknown tongues." Yost went to the Indian camps and told them that American reinforcements more numerous than the leaves on the trees were on their way to Fort Stanwix. The Indians believed Yost and melted away to their homes, leaving the Canadians no choice but to follow.

Returning to the main army, Arnold helped the American forces stand up to the best the British could do at an engagement at Freeman's Farm on September 19, 1777. The Americans had built strong defensive works, but experience had already shown that even the strongest works were susceptible to destruction by artillery fire. Once the protective earthworks were battered down, the British army would, as a rule, use its most effective tactic, a bayonet charge. Much of the American force was made up of militia, a group notorious for not having the training and discipline to stand up to either artillery fire or bayonets. It was Arnold's idea to advance from the defensive positions to meet the British in thick woods where a bayonet charge would not be feasible. Although the idea worked, the new American commander, Horatio Gates, distrusted Arnold as being too bold and took away his command. When General Gates wrote his official report of the action at Freeman's Farm, he did not even mention Arnold or his contribution to the American victory.

By now winter was approaching, and General Burgoyne was faced with two choices: break the American lines or retreat. Steadily increasing American numbers made the first impossible, but his pride prevented the second. Soon weather would prevent more supplies from arriving from Canada. The British forces in New York City had not moved to the aid of Burgoyne either.

On October 7, 1777, General Burgoyne attacked the American lines, and once more the Americans moved forward to meet the British troops. Hearing the sound of battle, Arnold borrowed a horse and rushed off to the fight, although without any troops under his command. Always heading into the hottest gunfire, Arnold electrified the American force with his extraordinary courage, energy, and seemingly invincible spirit. Soon officers as well as men were following his inspiring example. British and German troops were crushed, and in a final charge, a fortified position crucial to Burgoyne's force was captured. Just as his men poured into the redoubt, Arnold's horse was shot, and as it went down, a bullet shattered the rider's left leg, with the horse falling on top of the badly wounded man. A few days later Burgoyne accepted the inevitable, and his entire army surrendered to the Americans, largely as a result of Arnold's actions.

Later events would destroy Arnold's loyalty to America and would make him forever a traitor. He would again be passed over for promotion and recognition and would come increasingly under the influence of his pro-British wife. Disappointment and jealousy would cause him to betray military secrets to the British and accept a commission in the Royal Army. But his early patriotism was thought worthy of some recognition. Today, on the battlefield of Saratoga, at the place where Arnold went down with a disabling wound to his limb, there is a statue of a man's left leg inscribed with a single name—"Arnold"—a monument to a loyal leg.

"I Have Not Yet Begun to Fight" or Words to That Effect

The annals of the past resonate with the memorable words of famous people, but we contemporary citizens of the United States may wonder just how, in the midst of death and danger, our forebears were able to think up such appropriate words to be uttered in such dramatic circumstances. The truth may be that they didn't say those words at all; or if they did, they were not in the form we find so familiar and inspiring.

Of all the mottoes of the Revolution, none is more widely known than the reply made by Capt. John Paul Jones as he responded to a demand that he surrender his ship, *Bonhomme Richard*. When Captain Pearson of the Royal Navy's *Serapis* demanded he give up, Jones replied, "I have not yet begun to fight." Or words to that effect.

One of the problems to be overcome before the colonies could win their independence was the lack of a navy. With a long coastline to defend and the need to import manufactured goods from Europe, a navy was badly needed to patrol the coast and to convoy merchant ships. The Continental government did not have the money or the facilities to construct warships. As a result the Continental Navy was a rather ragtag affair.

But if the navy was lacking in material, it did have leaders like John Paul Jones, a man motivated by an overwhelming thirst for victory.

Following the alliance between the emerging United States and France in 1777, Jones began to hope that the new ally would provide ships and assistance to remedy the needs of the fledgling navy. In this hope he was partly justified.

In the spring of 1778, Jones had sailed from Boston aboard *Ranger*. This ship mounted eighteen cannons, but each gun fired a ball weighing only six pounds. This was too small to allow *Ranger* to fight most British naval vessels, so Jones stuck to commerce raiding. He carried the war to the home waters of Great Britain, capturing merchant ships while in full view of people on the beaches and mounting a raid on the town of Whitehaven. Such exploits made Jones a hero in France as well as in America.

With *Ranger* needing repairs and supplies, Jones entered the French port of l'Orient. Instead of repairs to his small ship, Jones was offered as a gift a large merchant ship and the means to convert her into a forty-gun frigate. Jones chose for his new command the name *Bonhomme Richard,* in honor of Benjamin Franklin, author of *Poor Richard's Almanac,* who, as American Ambassador to France, was instrumental in obtaining the ship.

Late in August 1779 Jones led a fleet of seven American and French ships to sea to continue his harassment of British commerce. Two of the ships were privateers and were not legally subject to Jones's orders. As events would prove, the other ship captains acted with a great deal of independence, often ignoring Jones.

As Jones put to sea, the crew of *Bonhomme Richard* was a preview of what the nation it represented would become. Aboard the frigate were Americans, Irish, English, Scots, Swedes, Norwegians, Portuguese, Swiss, Italians, and East Indians. All the marines onboard, 137 in all, were French.

On September 23, 1779, off the coast of Yorkshire, Jones caught sight of an important quarry. Spread over the sea were forty-one merchant ships sailing for Portsmouth from the Baltic Sea. Aboard they had the tar and ship's masts on which the

Royal Navy would depend for the next several months. But between Jones and the prize convoy were two British warships, *Duchess of Scarborough* and *Serapis*.

Serapis was a new frigate mounting fifty cannons, most of them larger than the guns carried on *Bonhomme Richard*. Leaving *Duchess of Scarborough* to one of the smaller ships, Jones steered for *Serapis*. Their encounter would become one of the legendary sea fights of the Revolutionary War, indeed, of all time.

The ships were about 12 miles apart when they first sighted each other in the early afternoon, but the wind was so light that they did not reach gunshot range until about six o'clock that evening.

The main armament of *Bonhomme Richard* was six 18-pounder cannons (they fired a ball weighing eighteen pounds). On the first or second broadside, two of these guns burst, killing and wounding a number of the crew members. The rest of the main battery was abandoned as being too dangerous to fire, and the surviving gun crews moved to an upper deck to help wherever they could.

With *Serapis* still firing twenty eighteen-pounders, as well as smaller cannons, Jones realized he needed to come close alongside his opponent and attack by boarding *Serapis* for hand-to-hand fighting. Captain Richard Pearson of the *Serapis* was anxious to avoid such a situation and to utilize the advantage his artillery gave him. Still, Jones was able to ram *Serapis* from astern, but the boarding party was forced back to *Bonhomme Richard*. At that point Captain Pearson recorded that he called on Jones to surrender. No reply was received according to his official report, and Jones's report does not mention the incident at all.

In subsequent maneuverings *Serapis* fouled *Bonhomme Richard*'s mizzen rigging, and the two ships became locked starboard to starboard, bow to stern. The heavier guns of *Serapis* steadily silenced the cannons of Jones's ship, but because they were locked so closely together, the British guns could not be elevated to fire on *Bonhomme Richard's* main deck and rigging. As American guns were silenced, their crews joined the French marines on deck and in the rigging, continuing to fight with muskets and hand-grenades, small, powder-filled iron shells. Again Captain Pearson called on Jones to surrender, and Jones replied "with the most emphatic negative" according to the official report.

After two hours, during which the two ships pounded each other at point-blank range, the tide of battle suddenly turned. A sailor named William Hamilton had taken a bag of hand-grenades and made his way to the very end of a yardarm, directly over the hatch leading to the main gun deck of the *Serapis*. Lighting the fuse to one of the rather crude bombs, he tossed it down the British hatch. A large explosion swept the gun deck, and an enormous pall of smoke rose above the scene. The grenade had exploded just as cartridges, cloth bags filled with gunpowder, were being distributed to the gun crews. A chain-reaction explosion killed more than twenty men and set *Serapis* on fire. Soon after, the British ensign fluttered down from the mast.

The next morning Jones moved all his men, including the wounded, to *Serapis* and watched as *Bonhomme Richard* sank beneath the waves, the victim of the damage received in the fight. That same day he wrote his official report of the battle. In 1785 he wrote a memoir of his service. In neither piece of writing do the words "I have not yet begun to fight" appear. Forty-six years after the battle Jones's lieutenant, Richard Dale, asserted these words had been Jones's reply to the first demand for surrender.

We are not really sure what words Jones uttered. His deeds speak for him.

Cussin' in German Does No Good

Sacre damn! Swine Hund! Ja, you, you badaut. Mein Gott, vat ist dis?" Often there was just such an explosion from Wilhelm Steuben while he was attempting to teach the elements of drill to the Continental Army camped at Valley Forge in the late winter and early spring of 1778. Like any good drill instructor, Steuben needed to make his feelings known in an emphatic fashion, and having served in various European armies all his life, he was well equipped to express his feelings. Unfortunately, his preparation did not include a knowledge of English, only German and French. No matter how vigorous his dressing down of soldiers, Steuben soon found cursing in German did no good. But his ability to teach soldiers how to drill did.

The Continental Army was made up of brave men, for the most part. By January 1778 some of these men had more than two and a half years of military service behind them, but they still had not learned how to be soldiers. The Continental forces walked from place to place, they did not march. As a result, units became scattered along their route and did not arrive on the battlefield as a cohesive unit. The men knew how to load and fire their weapons but not how to deliver volley fire from massed ranks. When protected by breastworks, as at Bunker Hill, the men fought hard and gave a good account of themselves. But in the open field the story was the same, time and time again. The better drilled, better disciplined British troops always carried the day, leaving the Continental forces to run away and try again at a later date.

George Washington and his commanders were well aware of the problems facing the army. Officers were encouraged to drill their men, but the officers were themselves untaught in military matters. Often these amateur officers drilled their men by reading commands from a drill manual they did not understand themselves. Even then, some of the officers used British manuals, others French, and some Austrian or German books. There were some higher-ranking officers with military training and experience, but they felt drilling troops was a duty for sergeants or officers of low rank. Because these men chose not to perform drill duty, the task went largely undone, with a lingering negative effect on the army.

The French had just become allies of the colonies following the victory at Saratoga in the early winter of 1777–1778, and they were now sending help to the Continental Army. One of the first types of aid to arrive were military engineers who would help the Continentals lay out fortifications and fieldworks. These French engineers were, without question, the best in the world for their day, but the best drill instructors were from the Prussian Army of Frederick the Great, who ruled a part of present-day Germany.

Or, perhaps, the best drill instructors were *not* in that army. Wilhelm Steuben had been a rising star in the army of Frederick the Great until just after 1761. At that time he had been a captain in rank and was the youngest aide-de-camp on the army staff. Then, something happened and Steuben lost his post. He held a variety of positions with minor princes in various German states, but in 1777 Steuben was looking for a job. The Comte de St. Germaine, French minister of war, heard that his old friend needed a position, and he knew that his ability was far above his military rank, so St. Germaine called in the Continental ambassador, Benjamin Franklin, and recommended that Steuben and Franklin meet.

Franklin and Steuben agreed that being presented as an out-of-work ex-captain would not sound very impressive no matter how good Steuben might be at his job. Therefore, the two agreed to style the new recruit Lt. Gen. Baron von Steuben, late of the Prussian Army. Late in the year 1777, Baron von Steuben arrived in America accompanied by a personal secretary, Pierre Duponceau, a private chef, and a greyhound named Azor. Meeting with a committee of the Continental Congress, Steuben won their support by making a sporting offer. Unlike most of the foreign officers who offered to fight only in return for handsome salaries, Steuben offered to serve without rank or pay until he had shown he could make a positive contribution to the cause of independence.

Washington welcomed Steuben to the camp at Valley Forge. While the new drill instructor looked over the army, the private chef toured the kitchen. Finding that the kitchen was nothing more than a campfire with a couple of kettles and a wooden spit, the chef promptly departed. Steuben stayed.

In less than a week, Washington and Steuben had agreed on a plan. Steuben would write out a lesson in one phase of necessary drill each night. The next morning, while clerks made copies of the lesson for each brigade in the army, Steuben would teach that lesson to a model company. That afternoon the members of the model company would teach the lesson to their units while Steuben rode about the camp supervising. By taking an active role in drilling the troops, Steuben hoped to emphasize to all officers how important the task was. The Continental Army was not learning drill just so it could look good on a parade ground, it was learning drill so it could fight effectively on a battlefield.

It was then that the custom of Steuben cursing in German began. The men learning the drill were anxious to master their lessons. They had seen on the battlefield how these skills could save their lives. Even so, mastering the intricacies of drill took practice. When a unit became confused and muddled in its drill, Steuben would curse them furiously and, in his excitement, would forget all his English, leaving the soldiers more amused than abashed at his tongue lashing. On one occasion Capt. Benjamin Walker of New York offered to translate what had just been said. From that point on Steuben's profanity became a part of a show that provided occasional relief from the seriousness of the task at hand. Steuben also recognized, and respected, the independent nature of the volunteer soldiers he was teaching. In a letter to a friend in Germany he noted, "If I say to a French or Austrian soldier 'Do this because I say so' he will do it, but these Americans will answer me 'Damn you, do it yourself.' But if I tell an American 'You ought to do it because of these reasons' he will do it and do it well."

In only ten days the Continental Army had learned so much and had so much improved its performance that Washington himself was amazed. In the spring of 1778, the British decided to evacuate Philadelphia, which they had taken the year before. As the British left, Washington attacked, and for the first time since the war had begun, the Continental forces fought the British to a standstill in open combat. So impressed were the British that they never again challenged Washington's force in the open.

As one soldier at Valley Forge put it, "Cussin' in German did no good but trainin' did."

Nimham's Indian Company

On August 31, 1778, a skirmish was fought that involved the most completely American of all the units in the Patriot army. Most of the men in this unit made the supreme sacrifice on this field of battle in defense of their country. Today, amid the crowds of people and the thunder of traffic in New York City, their bodies lie in a secluded area of Van Cortlandt Park near an area known as Indian Field. The Patriot soldiers who fell there were Native Americans of Nimham's Indian Company of Stockbridge, Massachusetts.

The decision of these men to support the Patriot cause was a complex one. The history of America from the time of the first English colony in Virginia was one of constant expansion, a never-ceasing quest for more land. An independent United States would continue this course so destructive to Indian culture. The government of Great Britain was more sympathetic to the Native Americans. In 1763, in response to resistance led by Chief Pontiac, the British king had established the Line of Demarcation, reserving all lands west of the highest crest of the Appalachian Mountains for the various Indian tribes. This action made supporting the British appealing when the American Revolution began, and most of the tribes along the frontier became pro-British.

The Iroquoian Confederation did not follow this pattern. In the early 1760s George Washington, while serving in the Seven Years' War (in America usually called the French and Indian

War), became close friends with Andrew Montour, the leader of the Delaware tribe, part of the Iroquois Confederation. In 1778 Andrew's son, John, commanded a company of Delawares in the Continental Army under Washington, and the friendly relations with that tribe had won support from members of other tribes in the Confederation, including members of the Mohican tribe, who still lived in the vicinity of Stockbridge, Massachusetts. These Native Americans had adopted many parts of the culture of their white neighbors and were thoroughly integrated into Massachusetts units in Washington's army.

It had long been a plan of Washington's to form a special unit of light infantry made up of frontier riflemen and Indians. This unit would specialize in scouting, skirmishing, and making raids on the British. During the winter of 1777–1778, while at Valley Forge, Washington had asked, and received, from Congress permission to form such a unit. In late June and early July 1778, the unit began to take shape.

Historians estimate that more than one hundred Native Americans from various tribes were serving in the army under Washington's direct command, while many others served in other Patriot organizations. Washington ordered the Indians in his command to be temporarily separated from their regular units and brought together into a special corps. The overall command of the light infantry would belong to Capt. Allen McLane. Capt. Abraham Nimham would command the largest unit of Indians, the Mohicans from Stockbridge. Indeed, Captain Nimham welcomed the assignment because it would bring together all the Stockbridge Mohicans then scattered among the various units, welding them into a single fighting force.

At this point in the war, the British army held New York City, having occupied it in August 1776, while Washington and the Patriot army made their headquarters several miles north at White Plains. The area between the two forces was a "no man's land" where clashes between small bodies of troops frequently occurred.

The "Indian Corps" Washington organized was described by an eyewitness as wearing "a shirt of coarse linen down to the knees." This was the hunting shirt used by all frontiersmen, regardless of race. Beneath the hunting shirt the Indian troops wore linen pants and deerskin moccasins. For weapons the men carried a bow and some twenty arrows and a musket. With the bow and arrows, they were capable of a much more rapid rate of fire than musket-bearing troops, and at the short range usually involved in an ambush, they were quite deadly. Most also carried a knife or a short axe, or tomahawk. A full-strength infantry company would have been made up of fifty men, but Nimham's Indian Company probably had forty men. Although few in number, these men were veterans. Some of the Stockbridge men had seen action as early as Bunker Hill in June 1775, while a considerable number had fought at Monmouth during the spring of 1778, when Washington had confronted the British as they withdrew from Philadelphia.

The British unit assigned to protect their front lines against Patriot marauders was the Queen's Rangers, commanded by Lt. Col. John Simcoe. All the enlisted men, and some of the officers, were Loyalists born in America. The Rangers were a mixed unit; some were infantry, others mounted dragoons, or cavalry, commanded by Banistre Tarleton. Not only were these men familiar with the countryside, many of them had experience in the rough-and-tumble small-scale warfare of the frontier. Surrounded as they were by a hostile Patriot population, the Queen's Rangers had gained a great deal of combat experience. They also knew that they could never return to their homes if they lost the war. In short, they were formidable fighters.

In July 1778 Daniel Nimham's Indian Company laid an ambush for the Queen's Rangers. It was only a lucky accident that both Simcoe and Tarleton escaped being caught in this trap and killed. Both men immediately began plotting revenge.

On August 31, 1778, Simcoe led 500 men out from the British lines along the Square Mile Road, toward the village of the same name. Almost half of the British force advanced west of Tribbet's Brook, while the rest moved along the Bronx River. Tarleton and the dragoons stayed on the flank.

The lay of the land allowed Nimham's company to spot the British along the brook, but those along the river were out of sight. Nimham's Indian Company moved to attack the British soldiers they could see, and soon a lively skirmish was underway. Then disaster struck. The remainder of the British under Simcoe closed in behind Nimham's force. As the Indians left the cover of stone walls and bushes to retreat, Tarleton charged with his cavalry. This was the moment in battle that cavalry on both sides wait for. So long as the infantry remained in ranks or behind cover, the horsemen could accomplish little. Once the infantry broke ranks or left cover, the cavalry held a great advantage. Men on foot with empty muskets were no match for horsemen swinging sabers and firing pistols. Nimham and his men fought as best they could, but in only a few minutes, thirty-seven members of the Indian Company, including Captain Nimham, were stretched on the ground, dead.

The most completely American unit in the Patriot army was wiped out on the battlefield. The bodies of these soldiers were collected by local farmers and buried in what has come to be called Indian Field. There they still lie today, silent witnesses to their devotion to the cause of independence.

Author's note: The area of Van Cortlandt Park occupied by ball fields and called Indian Field is not the burial site. The graves are located along an old lane, today merely a footpath, near the park nursery.

Gateway to Hell

By the standards of later wars, the armies of the American Revolution were of small size. Even so, the matter of dealing with prisoners often strained the resources of both sides. High-ranking officers might be allowed to give their parole, a promise not to fight again until properly exchanged. These men could then live at liberty on whatever scale their available money would allow and might even return to their homes. Enlisted men faced far different conditions. Captured members of the Royal Army might find themselves marched from place to place about the frontier as their Patriot captors tried to find a place where the captives could be fed, housed, and kept safe from rescue. This was the fate of the British and German soldiers under Gen. John Burgoyne, who surrendered at Saratoga, New York, in September 1777 to Gen. Horatio Gates and his Patriot forces. The arrangement under which Burgoyne's soldiers surrendered called for them to be marched to Boston. From that port they would be sent to England, never again to serve in America. The Congress realized that returning these troops to England would only release soldiers there to come to America, so various excuses were found to avoid returning Burgoyne's men. Over the two years following their surrender, these men were marched from Saratoga, New York, to Charlottesville, Virginia. One of these soldiers later described their wanderings as "a very great hardship." Some of these men, especially the Germans, gave up all hope of returning to their homes and, with some encouragement from their captors, began to develop an interest in the country where they were held prisoner. Some who were allowed to work for German settlers on the Pennsylvania and Virginia frontier fell in love, married, and settled in America.

Patriots who became prisoners of war found that the British did not have the luxury of space in which to imprison them, and they might be housed under very cramped conditions onboard a disabled ship. Although, no prisoner on either side enjoyed luxurious conditions, the prison hulks, as the disabled ships were called, were the worst of a bad lot, so bad that many called them the "gateway to hell."

Prison hulks offered the British military the solution to several problems relating to prisoners. Ships were built to accommodate large numbers of men, relative to their size. Anchored in a harbor or bay, the risk of escape from the ship was minimized because any break for freedom would have to be made by swimming. Because the ships were disabled, they could not be moved even if the prisoners did manage to overpower their guards. The ships were surrounded by water, so there was no shortage of that essential commodity; and the ebb and flow of the tide solved the problem of waste disposal.

The British ship *Jersey* was typical of dozens of prison hulks. In 1776 *Jersey* was a troop ship that arrived from Europe carrying 400 Hessians. Following the fighting around New York City, the ship was used as a hospital for British causalities. Once the city had been captured, a fire destroyed many of the warehouses so *Jersey* became a floating storehouse. In 1778 a final conversion began. The masts were removed from the ship, horizontal slits were cut into the hull to allow more air and light to reach each deck, and *Jersey* became a prison hulk anchored permanently off Long Island. Although 400 Hessian infantry had crossed the Atlantic aboard *Jersey,* the prison population soon surpassed that figure. By 1780 more than 1,400 captives were packed into her holds.

Not much imagination is needed to picture the conditions aboard the prison ship. Rats ran at will through piles of garbage and excrement that were only rarely shoveled overboard. The men were covered with fleas and lice so that all sorts of diseases, from typhus to dysentery to small pox, were rampant. Food was scarce at best and of the poorest quality. Guards sometimes amused themselves by tossing apples into the hold, touching off an outbreak of fighting among the inmates.

Even under such brutal conditions, it was considered inappropriate to unceremoniously dump the dead overboard. In an attempt to dispose of bodies with a modicum of dignity, each morning a boat carrying the dead from the previous twenty-four hours would be rowed to nearby sand flats, accompanied by a burial detail. There the bodies were hastily interred. All too often the next high wind would send waves over the shallow graves, floating bodies back to the vicinity of the ship. These bodies bobbed about on the tide, even while the prisoners lowered buckets to obtain drinking water.

A boat was allowed to come out to the hulk to sell prisoners small luxuries, but not many men had money, and those who did soon ran out, so there was little relief from the coarse food the jailers provided. The British government provided a specified amount of money for each prisoner per day. This amount would have purchased enough food to sustain life, but the actual purchasing was left up to the prison officials. All too many of these men followed the practice prevalent on *Jersey* and kept most of the money for themselves.

Medical care was worse than the food. Doctors were available only on rare occasions, and nursing had to be provided by other prisoners. There was no cure for most of the diseases prevalent aboard the hulks, and the only preventative measures would have required more space per person, better hygiene, and a sufficient supply of good food and clean water, none of which were made available. On some occasions those who offered medical care were suspected of being murderers who actually poisoned the sick to hasten their deaths.

A man who later would become one of the leading poets of the new nation, Philip Freneau, was briefly held on a prison hulk. In 1780 he published a poem, "The British Prison Ship," one verse of which says:

> Swift from the guarded decks we rush along
> And vainly sought repose—so vast our throng
> Three hundred wretches here, denied all light,
> In crowded mansions pass the infernal night;
> Some for a bed their tattered vestments join,
> And some on chests, and some on floors recline,
> Shut from the blessings of evening air,
> Pensive we lay with mangled corpses there;
> Meagre and wan and scorched with heat, below,
> We loomed like ghosts, ere death had made us so!

The only relief from unimaginable horrors aboard *Jersey* were the visits of three local women who brought clothing, bandages, and food to the hulk. Sarah Whaley, Margaret Whetten, and Mrs. Adam Todd spent so much of their own money on prisoner relief that after the war, ex-prisoners created a fund to help support the women in their old age.

The battlefield was, and is, a terrible place. Revolutionary War hospitals were filled with suffering, and soldiers would do almost anything to avoid being admitted to one. But either the battlefield or the hospital was better than passing through the "gateway of hell" as a prisoner on a hulk.

Delaware Daredevil

The Revolution was largely an infantryman's war, and only a few cavalry leaders gained any degree of fame. One who did, though now largely forgotten, was Capt. Allan McLane of Delaware, a man whose deeds made him the Delaware Daredevil.

Born in Philadelphia in 1746, McLane married Rebecca Wells of Kent County, Delaware, and called that place home for the rest of his life. When war came in 1775, McLane was ready and helped raise a group of men to join Washington's army. His first adventure came when Washington was attacked by the British on Long Island in August 1776. McLane and his Delaware men found themselves almost surrounded. Rather than surrender, they made a slashing attack that not only broke the British lines but allowed them to take twenty prisoners.

After participating in the winter campaign at Trenton and Princeton, McLane was commissioned a captain and sent home to Delaware to raise a company. Soon, he was back with ninety-four recruits for the army, men whose enlistment bonuses he had paid out of his own pocket. Mounting his men, McLane became the "eyes" of Washington's army as the Patriots tried, and failed, to protect their capital at Philadelphia. At the Battle of Germantown, McLane's cavalry broke the British picket line and allowed Washington to surprise the enemy, gaining an initial advantage only to see that advantage lost in a confusion of orders.

When Washington went into camp at Valley Forge for the winter of 1777–1778, it was McLane who daily nipped at the heels of any British who ventured out of Philadelphia, driving back their scouts and capturing their foraging parties. Occasionally, McLane was able to take badly needed food to the Patriot forces, but much more frequently, he was able to bring Washington the information he needed to thwart the British. Much of this information he got from spies inside the city.

As the long winter went on, it became clear that the Royal Army did not intend to hold Philadelphia. The position was difficult to supply and did not have the strategic value of New York City. To keep an eye on the British, and perhaps to catch them at a disadvantage, Washington sent General Lafayette with 2,500 men to an advanced position. General Howe decided to wipe out this exposed force before leaving Philadelphia and was in position to attack before Lafayette realized the danger. Only minutes before the attack was to be made, McLane dashed into the Patriot camp. With McLane as guide Lafayette snuck his men out of the nigh-fatal trap, sometimes passing so close the Redcoats could be heard talking among themselves.

Just before evacuating Philadelphia in the spring of 1778, the British staff officers gave an elaborate party to honor their commander, Gen. William Howe, who had been ordered to return to England. Just as the party was at its height, a tremendous furor arose in the British camp. McLane and his cavalry had decided to crash the party and dashed into the camp swinging camp kettles filled with gunpowder from their hands. Every time a horseman passed a campfire, a kettle landed in the flames, followed by a flash of light, a roar, and a cloud of smoke. Confusion quickly replaced gaiety as McLane's men disappeared back toward the Patriot lines. Two days later, as the British left the city, McLane and his men entered close enough behind the retreating Redcoats to take sixty prisoners.

Benedict Arnold, the wounded hero of Saratoga, was made military governor of the city. He and McLane were too much alike in temperament to get along and soon they clashed. Their disagreement was made worse when McLane learned that

Arnold was profiting from selling army goods to civilians, leaving the soldiers undersupplied. Perhaps hoping to get rid of McLane permanently, Arnold sent him on scouts into the most dangerous places possible. Each time, McLane came back with prisoners and information, and his reputation grew steadily. On one such occasion McLane was asked to meet a spy who was thought to be a double agent. Although the meeting sounded very much like a trap, McLane went, accompanied by only two men. Leaving these companions to watch the road back to the Patriot lines, McLane rode alone into the yard of the tavern where the meeting was to take place. No sooner had the spy begun to speak than McLane heard horses approaching from the British camp. Seeing his escape route was already blocked, McLane calmly waited until the British were at the gate to the tavern yard. Instead of surrendering, as was expected, he charged the gate, shot the officer in charge of the detail, and raced down the road. Fearing an ambush, the would-be captors let him go.

Still, the animosity of a senior officer is never a good thing, and McLane found himself passed over for promotion and assigned to routine duties.

Relief from the office routine and paper pushing came when Gen. Anthony Wayne proposed an attack on the strong British outpost at Stony Point. McLane was chosen to gather intelligence about the garrison and fortifications there. Disguising himself as a rude countryman, McLane accompanied a woman of the area who had received permission to go into the fort to visit her son. No one paid any attention to the country bumpkin who stared in apparent amazement at the military arrangements going on around him. The information McLane brought back from this daring reconnaissance made the Patriot attack a complete success. A few weeks later, McLane provided the information that helped "Light Horse Harry" Lee capture Paulus Hook. After both these successes, McLane was overlooked in the congratulations and received no rewards for his actions.

Other men might have become disgusted by such treatment, but McLane only looked for more work to do. He soon found that work in Virginia, where he was sent to act as a scout for Generals Steuben and Lafayette. While scouting in Virginia, McLane recognized the opportunity to concentrate all the Patriot forces against Gen. Lord Cornwallis, who was advancing north from the Carolinas. He made several risky trips across Virginia, Maryland, Pennsylvania, and New Jersey to arrange the southern movement of Washington's army. Additionally, McLane made one sea voyage to contact the French fleet commanded by Adm. Francois DeGrasse and to coordinate the movement of the fleet to block the entrance of Chesapeake Bay so Cornwallis could not escape by sea. In the course of this sail, McLane helped direct an attack on a British sloop-of-war, an attack that ended with the capture of the Royal Navy ship.

Somewhat worn out by all this action, McLane was discharged from the army on December 31, 1781, but he could not remain idle. He was soon in command of the militia of Kent County, Delaware, and made himself a terror to all the Tories in the area.

McLane had a distinguished career in Delaware politics after the war, holding numerous offices, including Speaker of the State House of Representatives. When the United States went to war with Britain again in 1812, McLane was too old to fight, but not to speak his mind. In 1814 the British captured the nation's capital and burned the White House and other public buildings. Hearing of the defeat of the American forces, McLane scornfully said, "If I had been there, the British would not have been able to have done it." Who can say the old Daredevil was wrong?

A Little Stroll

It had been quite a day for the loosely organized force of Overmountain Men. They had left their homes on the western frontier weeks before and had crossed the mountains eastward to defeat one of the British columns threatening the American settlements. They'd done more than defeat it, however. On October 7, 1780, the Patriot militia led by such men as Charles McDowell, Isaac Shelby, John Sevier, and William Campbell had completely wiped out the force of British regulars and militia led by Maj. Patrick Ferguson. Ironically, Ferguson's defeat came on a small elevation known as Kings Mountain.

As the sun set, the guns fell silent, and even the shrieks of the wounded were hushed. In the gathering gloom of the twilight, John Sevier approached one of his men, Joseph Greer. This young man, only twenty years old, had already seen a good deal of warfare and had fought in the front of the battle all day at Kings Mountain. If the British had failed to shoot him, it was their fault, for at seven feet tall and three hundred pounds, Greer provided an excellent target. But Sevier did not want Greer to fight anymore that day, he wanted him to travel.

The Patriot cause was not faring well. In the North the war had been at a stalemate ever since the spring of 1777, when Washington had fought the British to a standstill at Monmouth Courthouse in New Jersey. Since that time, the opposing armies had skirmished and maneuvered around New York City, but nothing seemed to happen to bring the war nearer to a close.

In the South the war had been an unmitigated disaster. Savannah and Charleston had fallen to the enemy, and the British cavalry under Banistre Tarleton ranged over the land at will.

The Congress in Philadelphia needed to hear some good news, as did all the supporters of the Patriot cause.

The request John Sevier made of Joseph Greer seemed a simple one. Would Greer take a little stroll up to Philadelphia and tell the Congress what the boys had accomplished at Kings Mountain? Greer's response to the request was to leave early on the morning of October 8.

Hundreds of miles of wilderness lay between Greer and the Congress. He could not turn east into the more settled area of the Carolinas, for that territory was in the hands of the British. The frontier, however, was flooded with Indians who were supporting the British in an attempt to stop settlers from moving west Greer would be in danger whichever way he went, but the frontier offered one advantage: Greer had been trading with the Indians all his life, and he knew their ways. So, along the frontier he went.

Steadily Greer traveled, constantly watching the woods around him for enemies. At night he was sometimes fortunate enough to find a log cabin with a friendly fire and hot food, where a traveler with news was welcome. Many nights his bed was the cold ground. Because he was such a large man, Greer's horse did not stand the strain of the journey for long, and when the mount went lame, no replacement could be found on any of the few frontier farms he passed. So Joseph Greer walked, his huge boots wearing out with every step.

Crossing rivers was bad. Cold weather had arrived, with frost every morning and occasional ice on puddles of water. The streams were frigid, and his clothes were slow to dry, but Greer kept on walking.

In southwestern Virginia the trip became even more dangerous. Greer saw the signs left by a band of Indians, little things such as broken twigs, slight impressions of feet in soft ground, the carefully hidden remains of small campfires. Then it happened. Looking down a long ridge as he checked his own back trail, Greer saw a group of Indians tracking him.

Running now, trying to put as much distance as he could between himself and the war party, Greer knew he was leaving plain signs for all his pursuers to follow, but he saw no alternative. Faintly, in the distance, he could hear war whoops, and he knew the chase was on.

All the rest of the day, Greer trotted on. Whenever a height allowed a look behind him, he saw Indians coming up his track. Ahead was a difficult stream crossing that Greer knew would slow him down, and he was getting tired. Then, an opportunity presented itself in the form of a fallen hollow sycamore tree. Greer dove into the cavity and then reached back outside to scatter leaves over the faint marks his entry had made. Now, it was a matter of luck.

The sudden stillness of the forest creatures told Greer his trackers were near. A little later, he could hear them talking. They were puzzled that they had lost his trail. A muted thump told Greer one of his pursuers was sitting on the log in which he was hidden. Even after the birds began chirping again, Greer lay still. It was the next morning before he crawled out of his log.

Somewhere in the Shenandoah Valley some days later, Greer got another horse. Travel was still dangerous, but there were more people here, and he traveled wore quickly. In Maryland and Pennsylvania it was safe for him to move east, and Greer could move faster yet. At last, Philadelphia came into view.

Greer truly stood out in these surroundings. Not only did he tower above everyone else, he looked like a wild man. His hair was long and tangled, as was his beard. He was wearing the same clothes in which he had fought at Kings Mountain, and they had not been in the height of eastern fashion even when new. Like most of his frontier peers, Greer was wearing a hunting shirt. This was a one-piece, long-sleeved garment made of cloth woven from linen and wool that hung straight from the shoulders to the knees. A leather belt caught the shirt at the waist, likely with a knife or a tomahawk—or both—thrust into the belt. Beneath the hunting shirt, short breeches with leggins replacing stockings disappeared into boots or high-topped moccasins. A broad-brimmed felt hat topped off the ensemble. In Greer's case the entire outfit was ragged from wear and stained from travel. Although his body and his clothes were dirty, his long rifle was gleamingly clean.

Ignoring the stares, Greer made directly for the statehouse, whose clock tower rose above the surrounding roofs, on Chestnut Street. Up the steps he strode, his "little stroll" almost over. Old Andrew McNair was charged with the duty of doorkeeper for the Congress and was decidedly of the opinion that the wild man pacing down the corridor did not belong there, but when a wild man is seven feet tall and carrying weapons with which he seems familiar, discretion is a recommended course.

With a dignity born of a purpose fulfilled, Greer walked up to the speaker's table. "Sirs," he said, "I am just come from the Carolina backwoods bearing great good news. God has blessed us with victory."

Some years later, Greer was awarded 3,000 acres of land in Lincoln County, Tennessee, as a reward for his services. Greer is buried on that farm, and his large boots are on display in the Tennessee State Museum in Nashville.

Sharks in the Harbor

The British army captured New York City in August 1776 and held it until the end of the war. Its magnificent harbor made the city the major point of entry for supplies for the Royal Army, and the supplies attracted Patriot raiders. Throughout the war, these raiders darted like sharks through the harbor, striking merchant ships, seizing valuable cargoes, and disappearing into the inlets and creeks along the New Jersey shore. These daring attacks were not made in conventional warships but were often launched by men operating in rowboats. These rowboats were commonly carried aboard whaling ships that were used to chase and kill whales. Obviously, such boats had been designed to be quite seaworthy and could carry a fairly large number of men. Typically, the boats were double-ended, 26 to 30 feet in length, and capable of carrying up to twenty-four men. The only armament attached to the boat was a swivel gun, a small weapon mounted on a pivot and most effective when used as an oversized shotgun at close range. A successful attack depended on the rowboats closing swiftly on the target, like a shark, and the crew charging onto the decks of the target vessel armed with cutlasses and pistols to overwhelm its crew.

Although the Royal Navy used warships to protect convoys crossing the ocean, there were not enough ships and men to protect vessels once they had entered the sheltered waters of a harbor, nor could the navy guard the numerous small craft that flitted about the harbor going about their various tasks. These conditions gave the Patriot raiders their chance.

The swiftest sharks in New York harbor were William Marriner and Adam Hyler, both of New Brunswick, New Jersey. Marriner was a tavernkeeper. He used his barroom as a collecting point for news about British ships entering the harbor that might be anchored in isolated, vulnerable spots while awaiting openings at the docks. On April 18, 1780, Marriner heard of a desirable prize, but it was questionable as to whether it was in a vulnerable position.

The *Blacksnake* was a brig that had been fitted out as a commerce raider by a group of Rhode Island businessmen. These private warships, or privateers, could be a profitable investment because all ships and cargoes they captured became the property of the captors. Unfortunately for the Rhode Island group, *Blacksnake* had been captured by the British almost as soon as she had put to sea. Now, she was lying at anchor at Sandy Hook in the shadow of a British ship-of-the-line, *Volcano*, which mounted seventy-four heavy cannons.

Taking only nine men with him, and ignoring the odds, Marriner steered his boat through the night. With its oars padded with leather so as to make no sound, the small boat stole past *Volcano* and swept under the stern of *Blacksnake.* Without a sound, the attackers swept over the decks of the brig, overpowering the watch on duty and capturing the off-duty watch asleep. There was no time to raise the anchor, so Marriner cut the cable with an ax and headed out to sea in a direction opposite than that which the British were expecting. By the time sailors on *Volcano* noticed the movements aboard *Blacksnake,* the brig was fading into the darkness. By the time the alarm had been sounded and guns loaded, *Blacksnake* had disappeared completely. The next morning, *Blacksnake* sighted a schooner heading for New York and gave chase. By midday Marriner sailed into Toms River, New Jersey, with not just his newly captured privateer, but with a prize to be sold as well.

This success made Marriner a marked man. Within a year the British had captured him, but he was released on parole, with a promise he would not fight again. Soon, his place as leader of the sharks was taken by Adam Hyler.

Hyler was an immigrant from Germany who owned a small fleet of trading vessels when the war began. The skills Hyler had learned sailing his trading fleet along the Atlantic coast stood him in good stead in his career as a harbor shark.

On the night of October 5, 1781, Hyler left New Brunswick with his small sloop, *Revenge,* towing two rowboats. His destination was Sandy Hook, where five British merchant ships rocked peacefully at anchor, guarded by a British man-of-war in the harbor and a log and sand fort on the shore.

Anchoring off the entrance to the bay, Hyler sent in one rowboat to scout the situation. Hyler waited, not too patiently, for the return of his scout. Finally, the boat returned and reported no signs of life, even aboard the guard ship. Hyler assigned his rowboats to take the four smaller merchant vessels, while he led *Revenge* to capture the better-armed larger ship. Despite the darkness, all the targets were struck at nearly the same moment. Using only cold steel, the attackers overwhelmed the crews without a sound, although a few men escaped in the ships' lifeboats or by swimming. Knowing the alarm would soon be given ashore, Hyler got everything underway as quickly as he could, but not soon enough to escape cleanly. Firing broke out from the fort, and though the shots all went wide of the mark, the guard ship was alerted. The most valuable cargo was stripped from the merchant ships and piled aboard *Revenge,* and then the captured ships were set afire. In the blaze of the next noonday, Hyler sailed into the harbor of New Brunswick to be hailed as a hero.

A successful career as a harbor shark made Hyler and his home port of New Brunswick a target for the British. On January 7, 1782, a raiding party swept into the town and burned the fleet of small boats used by the Patriots. Hyler was not deterred from his career, only angered at what had happened. Finding another boat, he disguised his men as British sailors and boldly rowed across the harbor to Manhattan, hoping to kidnap some of the officers who had raided his home. Bad luck seemed to dog the expedition, however, for there was a grand social event in New York that night, and all the men Hyler had wanted to capture were not at home, having gone to the party. On his way back home, however, Hyler saw a sloop loaded with cargo just entering the harbor. Not content to go back empty-handed, he led his men in a surprise attack that left the ship and its contents in his hands.

This was one of the last exploits of Adam Hyler. On September 6, 1782, he suddenly became severely ill and died the same day. Ten days later, his wife gave birth to a son, Adam, Jr., who would one day becoming a seafaring man himself.

The sharks in the harbor were no substitute for a Patriot navy, but they succeeded in making life miserable for the British sailors who dared come their way.

The Georgia War Woman

In Elbert County, Georgia, there is a small stream named War Woman's Creek, a name which keeps alive the memory of Nancy Hart, a legendary Amazon warrior of the frontier. Some would argue that the Nancy Hart story is primarily legend because nothing about her exploits appeared in print until fifty years after the Revolution. This time lapse certainly would allow for imagination to color the memories of those who knew Nancy Hart, but beginning in the 1830s, sound historical research that has not been contradicted laid a basis of fact about Nancy.

Nancy Morgan was born about 1735 on the Pennsylvania frontier, and her family, like so many other frontier families, followed the wall of the Appalachian range of mountains south to the Carolinas. There she married Benjamin Hart. By 1771 they had moved across the Broad River into Georgia. By this time the couple was well on their way to having eight children, all of the family living in a one-room cabin with a loft in which the children slept.

Often legends depict all frontier women as beautiful, but life on the frontier was hard, and Nancy's face and figure showed the effects of a difficult life that included many hours of hard work every day, as well as bearing a large number of children. A contemporary described her as "cross-eyed, with a broad, angular mouth, ungainly in figure and rude in speech, standing about 6 feet in height and rather muscular." Nancy's speech was called "rude" in the polite euphemism of the eighteenth century; today, it would be called crude or vulgar. Nancy, by all accounts, could curse like a mule skinner. Despite being cross-eyed, she was a good shot and contributed to the family larder by hunting alongside her husband.

When the Revolution began, Benjamin became an officer in the Georgia militia. For the first three years of its course, the war was fought primarily in New England and the mid-Atlantic states, but beginning in 1778 the war moved south. The British thought they might split off a section of the colonies and keep them under Royal control, even if they were to lose New England. The presence in the southern colonies of a large number of Loyalists, or Tories as they were called by their Patriot neighbors, supported British hopes for success. By 1780 the situation of the Patriots was becoming severe. The British had captured Savannah, Georgia, and Charleston, South Carolina, forcing the only large Patriot army in the south to surrender. The victorious Royal army then moved inland toward the frontier, sweeping west and northwest, hoping to wipe out all support for the cause of independence. These successes encouraged the Tories and persuaded many fence-sitters to go over to the British side. So many people came flocking to the Royal standard that, at times, there were more Americans fighting against independence than there were fighting for it. Under these circumstances the war in the south became a bitter struggle between former friends, neighbors, and even relatives. In many ways the War for Independence had become a civil war. The Hart family was in the middle of this sort of conflict.

While her husband led the Patriot militia from their area into the field to fight, Nancy tried to help the cause by going on a mission to gain desperately needed information about the British plans. Nancy took on the role of a half-wit peddler and entered the British lines at Augusta, Georgia, selling pies. She was so convincing a half-wit that no one paid her any attention, and she gathered the desired intelligence.

Even when her husband was away, the Hart cabin was open to Patriot scouts and spies, who always found Nancy ready to offer a meal, a roof over their heads, and a corn-shuck mattress on the loft floor. This sort of activity did not escape the notice of the British and their Tory allies. In 1781 six of the Tories paid Nancy a fatal call.

Hoping to disrupt the Patriot militia, the Tories made a raid out of Augusta into the neighborhood where the Hart family lived. Some militia members were killed, and others escaped into the woods. In the late afternoon the Tory party reached the Hart cabin. Benjamin and the older boys were still working in the cornfields, so only Nancy and the girls were at home.

Riding into the yard, the raiding party demanded food. When Nancy argued that the family barely had enough to feed themselves, the raiders shot a turkey that was standing in the barnyard and ordered her to cook that. Cursing, Nancy called her oldest daughter and loudly told her to go to the spring for more water. Quietly, she told the child to go to the field and warn her father and brothers so they could gather some of the neighbors. Nancy, of course, worked as slowly as she could to give the men time to gather.

While waiting for the turkey to roast, the Tory raiders began to relax with a jug of homemade whiskey, a commodity found in almost every frontier cabin. As the level of the liquid in the jug went down so did the level of alertness displayed by the men. While moving about the cabin preparing food, Nancy began to slip their guns out the window, where another of her children took them. Several of the weapons had been spirited away when one of the Tories saw Nancy with his musket in her hands. He shouted a warning to the others and Nancy, unhesitating, shot him through the heart. Dropping the empty musket, she caught up another and put another raider on the floor. Quickly, another weapon was in her hands.

"Stay still or you are all dead men," she said. There were more men on their feet than there were muskets still in the room, but no one wanted to find out who would be left standing after the last shot had been fired. The standoff ended when Benjamin and several neighbors arrived.

The discussion of what to do with the prisoners ended when Nancy gruffly said, "Hang them." Within a few minutes all the surviving Tories were swinging at the end of a rope, victims of the rough justice often meted out on the frontier.

In the 1950s a rail line was being built through the area once occupied by the Hart cabin. Archaeologists excavating the site in advance of the construction crew were surprised to find human bones. At the conclusion of their work, they had recovered parts of six skeletons. There had been six members of the raiding party. Nancy Hart truly deserves her reputation as "The Georgia War Woman."

The Meanest Man in America

The British lieutenant colonel gazed intently down the length of the grassy field. There was a solid line of Rebel infantry down there, but none were wearing uniforms because they were just militia. He knew what would happen. He and his men would go at them at a gallop. At about 70 yards the militia would fire, and he would lose a handful of men and horses. The militia would then drop the butts of their muskets to the ground so they could reload, but before that task could be completed, his dragoons would be among the Rebels, sabers slashing. It would be a massacre, as usual.

Tugging his green uniform jacket into a comfortable position, Banistre Tarleton turned to his bugler and said, "Sound the charge."

On battlefield after battlefield, both in the northern theater and in the South, the dragoon troops under Banistre Tarleton carved their way to victory with the saber, splashing blood across the pages of the history of the Revolution. No other soldiers on either side earned so high a reputation for effective fighting or so low a name for viciousness. Was Tarleton really the meanest man in America?

Banistre Tarleton was born to a middle-class family in England, but his father had earned a fair fortune and was able to send his sons to a university. Although Tarleton enrolled to study law, he was much more interested in gambling, drinking, and visiting with ladies than he was in studying. Leaving the university without a degree, Tarleton inherited the large sum of 5,000 pounds sterling from his father's estate. In a short time he had gambled away the entire sum and, to have some means of living, purchased a commission as an ensign, a low-ranking officer, in the fashionable First Dragoon Guards. Not much attracted to the routine of garrison life, Tarleton volunteered for service in America on December 25, 1775.

Almost as soon as he landed in the rebellious colonies, Tarleton began to make a name for himself. On December 13, 1776, he was in the party of cavalry that captured Gen. Charles Lee, the commander of a major part of the Continental Army. Throughout 1777 he rode at the head of his unit as the dragoons scouted and fought with Washington's Patriot army. Following the capture of Philadelphia, Tarleton was always to be found at the center of parties and balls. All the while, the Patriots shivered and trained in their barren camp at Valley Forge.

In the spring of 1778, the British found the Patriot army to be their equal in battle, but Tarleton's star still shone bright. In the reorganization of the British forces following the Battle of Monmouth Courthouse, Tarleton was promoted to the staff position of brigade major.

As the British army settled into New York City—for the remainder of the war, it turned out—Tarleton was authorized to recruit a unit of cavalry from among Americans loyal to the Crown. Soon after this, he was allowed to recruit some light infantry companies that, combined with his cavalry, became the "British Legion." Except for a few officers, all the men in this unit were from America.

The war around New York City did not offer much for Tarleton and his men. In 1779 his unit became a part of the British force sent south to try to win the war in an area that had seen but little fighting. The arrival of the British Legion and its commander in the South was not auspicious. The unit had no horses; all 300 of their mounts had died aboard ship during transit.

As soon as he and his men took horses from Patriot farmers, Tarleton and the legion began to establish a bloody reputation. There had been almost no fighting in the South, and the Patriot forces there lacked the combat experience of their northern counterparts. Tarleton won some easy victories against these raw troops. The defining moment of Tarleton's career came on May 29, 1780, at a settlement called Waxhaws on the North Carolina–South Carolina border. Col. Abraham Buford's regiment of Virginia Continentals was escorting Gov. Archibald Rutledge of South Carolina, who had barely escaped capture at Charleston. At Waxhaws, Buford was brought to battle. Offered a chance to surrender, the Virginian refused. Tarleton then charged, and many Continentals were killed after throwing down their muskets and asking for "quarter," or mercy. "Tarleton's Quarter" became a chilling battle cry meaning "take no prisoners." Tarleton pointed out, as his defenders have done since, that having refused to surrender when called on, the Patriot forces had given up all rights to protection under the existing laws of war. When a defending force chose to continue fighting after being summoned to stop, the attacking force was not then required to take prisoners. Although the fine points of the law might be on Tarleton's side, the Patriots saw only a bloody-handed man who was now fair game for anyone who could get him in the sights of a rifle.

After the Waxhaws fight, Tarleton and his men became a terror to the Patriot forces. Cavalry was a very effective arm of the military during the Revolutionary War because of the limited range of infantry weapons. The cavalry was not in range of musket fire until a distance of about 80 yards was reached. Once the cavalry passed that mark, the infantry could fire only one shot per soldier before the cavalry covered the remaining distance, catching the infantry with unloaded muskets. If the infantry had proper training, discipline, and were armed with bayonets, the foot soldiers could still defend themselves with empty muskets. But the Patriot forces confronting Tarleton had none of these things.

Following the Battle of Camden, Tarleton again pursued the defeated Patriots, wreaking havoc. He and his men fought numerous skirmishes with guerrilla leaders Francis Marion and Thomas Sumter, but these engagements eventually proved to be Tarleton's undoing. The more the Patriots fought, the more skilled at arms they became. When the Battle of Cowpens was fought, the Patriots' fighting skills were equal to or better than those of Tarleton's men. As the British moved north from the Carolinas into Virginia, following their defeats at Cowpens and Kings Mountain, Tarleton and the British Legion still led the way, they still won battles, but they also suffered defeats. Their skill as fighters was still strong and their use of the saber no less fearsome, but after Cowpens the Patriots were no longer terrified of either.

The end of his American career came for Tarleton at Yorktown. As Lord Cornwallis waited in vain for rescue by the Royal Navy, Tarleton was sent across to the north side of the York River to keep the Patriot and French forces from getting too close to the British rear. While out on a foraging expedition for corn, Tarleton was attacked by a squadron of French cavalry and was wounded. On October 19, 1781, along with the rest of the British forces, Tarleton surrendered, giving himself up to the French. He feared the Americans would give him "Tarleton's Quarter." They thought Banistre Tarleton was the meanest man in America.

The Old Wagon Driver

The whip came whistling down and cracked across the bloody, raw back of the young colonial dangling by his wrists from the tripod. "Five hundred," said the drum major.

"No, it's not," thought the barely conscious victim. "It's only 499. That's one lash left, but instead of taking it, I'll give it. One day I'll pay you Lobsterbacks with interest." In 1781 Daniel Morgan would do just that; indeed, he would give the British army "a devil of a whipping" at Cowpens, South Carolina.

Morgan received his flogging at the hands of the British Army during the Seven Years' War, during which he served as a wagon driver, hauling supplies for the army. A dispute arose between Morgan and a young officer. Morgan's behavior was judged to be insubordinate, and the officer ordered punishment. This kind of treatment helped convince Morgan that independence and self-government might be a good idea.

During the tumultuous years between 1761, when the Seven Years' War ended, and 1775, Morgan lived on his farm in Frederick County, Virginia, and supplemented his income by keeping a tavern. He also became a leading local spokesman for independence.

When the conflict with Britain began in 1775, Morgan took decisive action, raising a company of riflemen to serve at the siege of Boston. He later led his frontier marksmen in action at Quebec and Saratoga. Although a devoted and skillful soldier, Morgan was passed over for promotion time and again. His humble background, a source of pride for him, prevented the leaders in Congress from seeing his worth and ability. Finally, disgusted with his treatment, Morgan returned to his home in July 1779 and went back to farming. In August 1780 the Patriot army in South Carolina suffered a crushing defeat at Camden, leaving all the southern states open to British invasion. In the face of this emergency, Morgan rejoined the army.

The new Patriot commander in the South was Gen. Nathanael Greene. This Rhode Island native recognized the innate talent of Morgan and gave him command of half the army. The army was quite small, however, and this grand-sounding command actually meant Morgan had only about nine hundred men under him.

Greene made a bold decision as he surveyed the strategic situation. Although his army was smaller than the British force under Lord Cornwallis, Greene separated his forces. Morgan, with his half of the army, was sent to the west to hold in check the British attempts to expand on the frontier. Greene stayed in the east with a slightly larger force. If Cornwallis moved ahead in the middle, both Morgan and Greene would close in behind him. If Cornwallis attacked Greene, Morgan could counterattack on the frontier. If Cornwallis came after Morgan, Greene would be free to move on Charleston. This plan had a potential for success, but it was risky. Cornwallis, by a bold move, might manage to pin down and defeat the smaller Patriot units one at a time.

Confronting Morgan was the British cavalry leader Banistre Tarleton, a fierce man who commanded a mixed force of infantry, cavalry, and artillery. Many of Tarleton's soldiers were Loyalists from New Jersey and New York.

Morgan commanded a small group of Patriot regulars—Continentals—from Maryland and Delaware, and a larger body of militia from North Carolina, Georgia, South Carolina, and Virginia. Some of the militia had no combat experience, and Morgan was uncertain of their fighting ability, but many of the militiamen were veterans who had served a term as Continentals and had then reenlisted in the militia.

In a move much like poking a hornet's nest with a stick, Morgan sent his cavalry under William Washington to attack British foraging parties and to wipe out small outposts. The cavalry attacks had the desired effect, and soon Banistre Tarleton was pounding down the available roads in pursuit of the Patriot forces.

Morgan was ready to fight Tarleton, but he knew he had to find the proper location. If there were swamps or heavy woods for cover, his raw militia would melt away to be seen no more. If the ground were too open, Tarleton's horsemen would sweep around his flanks and overrun his men from the rear. So Morgan fell back, all the while looking for a place to fight. He found that place at Cowpens on January 17, 1781.

Cowpens was an open grazing ground where cattle were allowed to roam freely. The browsing animals kept down undergrowth and provided open views in all directions over several acres of ground. Also, the terrain gradually swept up toward a crest as one moved into the area. Morgan liked the location immediately. He could have his men under visual observation, and they would have clear fields of fire, but there were no swamps or thickets to tempt the raw militia to run for cover.

Morgan's plan took advantage of the strengths of his men and minimized their weakness. The smallest group of militia, men from North Carolina and Georgia under Col. Charles McDowell, were placed in the front line. These men were told they were expected to fire two shots and then they were free to retreat. They were specifically asked to fire at British officers. Because many of these men were armed with rifles, they could fire at a long range and be safely out of the way of the enemy before the British came close enough for a bayonet attack. A second line of more experienced militia under Colonel Pickens would also damage the British advance with two shots before falling back behind the main line, which was composed of Continentals and seasoned militia under Colonel Howard and Major Triplett. William Washington had about one hundred twenty-five cavalry in reserve.

Banistre Tarleton, in his typical fashion, marched his men all night in order to close in on the enemy. When the Patriot position was sighted, an attack was ordered without scouting. Tarleton expected his usual success against militia. When the British approached the advanced Patriot line under McDowell, many of the men fired several shots before falling back instead of only the two requested by Morgan. Many of the shots took British officers out of action—some reports say as many as 30 percent of the commanders fell. As McDowell's line fell back, the advance of the British inevitably became disordered as some men went forward faster than others. Colonel Pickens's experienced line was something of a surprise to these men, so Tarleton ordered a charge of his cavalry, his superweapon that had brought him victory so often before. This time the British cavalry met a countercharge by Colonel Washington, and the Patriot dragoons swept the field.

With his cavalry in disarray, Tarleton still had to face the final line, the Continentals and Virginia militia. An exchange of musket volleys was followed by a bayonet charge by the Patriots. Fifteen minutes after the first shots were fired, the British survivors were in full flight. Tarleton had lost 841 out of 936 men. The Old Wagon Driver had paid back the missing lash—in Tarleton's own words, Morgan had delivered "a devil of a whipping."

I Can Fire a Cannon at It If I Want–It's My House

The bright blue sky arching above Yorktown belied the turmoil going on around the little village of sixty or so houses and a few public buildings. Once an important port on the York River, the village had become a quiet backwater until recently. Then, the armies—British, Continental, and French—had arrived. Now, the place was anything but quiet. Yorktown stood on a bluff across a half-mile of river from Gloucester Point. On each side of the village were deep ravines through which creeks flowed to join the York River. Bulging out from the village in an arc to the west, south, and east, connecting the creeks, was a strong line of fortifications with both flanks anchored at the river. These were the positions of the British army commanded by Lord Cornwallis, who was hoping the British navy would sail up the river to rescue him and his men.

The line of British fortifications included seven redoubts, or enclosed earthen forts, and six fortified gun batteries, all connected by entrenchments for infantry. In front of the lines, rows of sharpened stakes, called abatis, were driven into the ground facing outward. Alert sentries kept close watch over the parapets, and gunners had lengths of slow-burning cord, or slow-match, ready to fire the cannons in the batteries should a hostile move be made.

Some half-mile outside the British lines was another bow enclosing the first. This raw pile of freshly turned dirt marked where the French and Continental soldiers had dug their first "parallel," their opening step in the siege of Yorktown. Now, shovels were flinging up more dirt as gun batteries were constructed, so that heavy cannon could begin battering away at the British defense lines.

Among those watching these developments with great interest was Thomas Nelson, a prominent citizen of Virginia. The Nelson family had been prominent in Virginia politics for a long time; indeed, William was elected to the lower house of the colonial legislature, the House of Burgesses, when he was only twenty-one years old in 1761.

The year 1761 marked the end of the Seven Years' War, also called the French and Indian War, and the beginning of troubles between Great Britain and the thirteen American colonies. Britain was the big winner in the war, depriving France of all its North American lands, but the debts accumulated during the war caused a series of crises over the issue of who should levy the taxes to pay the debts. The question raised was: Should the colonies tax themselves to help pay the debt or should the taxes be imposed by the British Parliament? The crises included disputes over the "Line of 1763" (which reserved all lands west of the crest of the Appalachians for the Indians), the Sugar Act, the Stamp Act, and the Townsend Duties (which included the infamous tax on tea). With each of these events, Thomas Nelson became more alienated from the motherland and more convinced the colonies should be independent and in control of their own destiny. Indeed, when resistance to tea carrying the British tax reached its peak, Nelson was among a group of men who boarded merchant ships at anchor at Yorktown, and he, personally, threw overboard two chests of tea.

Not surprisingly, Thomas Nelson was elected a member of the Continental Congress in 1775. He carried to that body's meeting in Philadelphia a document called the "Virginia Resolves," which urged the Congress to declare independence. Of course, Nelson signed the Declaration of Independence. Returning to Virginia in the spring of 1777, Nelson was active in the state legislature, in financing the war, and in recruiting men both for the Continental Army and the Virginia militia. In 1777, and again from 1779 to 1781, he served as commander of the Virginia militia. This public service was rewarded with election to the office of governor of Virginia in June 1781.

The state Nelson was chosen to lead was under the gun when he took office. The British army under Lord Cornwallis was flooding north across the state after cutting a swath of destruction across the Carolinas. The British threat was so great that the state government had abandoned its capital at Richmond and had moved across the Blue Ridge Mountains to Staunton. But events were about to take a dramatic turn.

The Continental forces in Virginia were led by the Marquis de Lafayette. His army was too small to confront Cornwallis directly, but with the help of the Virginia militia, it harassed the invaders and forced them to keep their forces in one body instead of fanning out across all the state. After doing as much damage as he thought possible, Cornwallis headed for a rendezvous with the navy on the coast. The chosen site was Yorktown. As soon as the British forces were committed to their course of action, the Continental and French forces began to concentrate against them. While Lafayette held the British in place, French soldiers moved southward from Providence, Rhode Island, and Washington led his Continentals from New York, across New Jersey, and down Chesapeake Bay. Sailing north from the Caribbean, a French fleet barred the entrance to Chesapeake Bay to the British ships coming to the aid of their embattled army. By late September the noose was drawing tight; Cornwallis was trapped at Yorktown.

Now, as the guns made ready to open fire on the British lines, dignitaries came pouring into the Continental positions to observe the ceremonial firing of the first shot. Gen. George Washington stepped forward and touched the glowing slow-match to the vent hole of a large cannon. The gun thundered, and smoke filled the battery while a twenty-four-pound iron ball sped toward the British lines.

Then, the governor of Virginia stepped forward. "That house over there makes a good target. I would not be surprised to find that it is Cornwallis's headquarters. Aim a cannon at that house, and let me fire a shot."

"Sir," the gunner replied, "General Washington is a military man. It is appropriate he should fire a shot, but I question the propriety of you, a civilian, being allowed to destroy civilian property. Such acts are inevitable but should be done only by the military."

"I think it would be all right for me to fire a cannon at that particular house," said the governor. "I live there." And a moment later Gov. Thomas Nelson sent a cannonball smashing into the wall of his own home. Eight days later Cornwallis surrendered.

Author's note: The Thomas Nelson House is now part of the Yorktown Colonial National Park and has been restored to its appearance at the time of the war. The town is surrounded by the reconstructed earthworks erected during the siege of 1781.

The Battle of the Bluffs

Charlotte Robertson was not surprised when the sound of three gunshots came echoing across the clearing around the little wooded stockade on the bluff above the Cumberland River. Nor was she frightened by the wild war cries coming from the warriors who were running back beyond gunshot range. Charlotte was a frontier woman, and it would take more than noise to frighten her.

The little stockade was called Nashboro (now Nashville, Tennessee), and its main attraction was a salt spring nearby. The fort had stood on the bluff above the Cumberland for only a year on that morning of April 2, 1781. The settlement was the farthest flung white outpost on the western frontier.

In 1776, when the Revolutionary War began, the Cherokee Indians had taken the side of the British in an attempt to stop the constant westward movement of settlers. All along the frontier the Patriot farmers responded with fierce attacks on Indian settlements. By the winter of 1776–1777, the Indian towns east of the Appalachian Mountains were little more than piles of ashes as their shivering, starving former inhabitants went as refugees into the mountains to try to eke out enough food to survive the winter.

Some of the Cherokee leaders had had enough of war and made an uneasy peace with the frontiersmen, but Dragging Canoe would have no compromise with the whites. Taking the most aggressive members of the Cherokee tribe with him,

Dragging Canoe moved to the banks of the Tennessee River and established new towns from Chickamauga Creek south to Nika-jack Cave. There he was joined by disgruntled members of other tribes. Soon, the Chickamaugas, as the inhabitants of these towns were called, became known as the most hostile and warring of all the Indians on the southwestern frontier.

In the summer of 1779, two settlers, James Robertson and John Donelson, decided to leave their homes in East Tennessee in the Watauga settlements and move to the fertile lands they had heard about in the middle part of what would become the state of Tennessee. Robertson would lead a band of men and boys driving livestock for the new settlement, while Donelson would bring another contingent by flatboat carrying heavy bulk goods. All the women and children, including James Robertson's wife, Charlotte, would travel with the Donelson party.

On March 8, 1780, the Donelson flotilla reached the country of the Chickamaugas. They had floated far down the river through the Chickamauga territory when, near present day Chattanooga, Indians in canoes began to put out from the banks to chase the clumsy flatboats. A moving fight began with all aboard rowing or fighting, or both. Several of the women took part in the battle. On the boat of Abel Gower, Charlotte Robertson's son-in-law, several of the men were wounded, and the boat was drifting dangerously near to shore when young Nancy Gower seized the rudder and steered back to midstream. It was not until the skirmish ended that Charlotte noticed that her granddaughter's dress was soaked with blood. Nancy had been shot in the thigh but had made no mention of the fact so long as the fight continued.

Jonathan Jennings's boat was overrun by the Indians when it struck a rock and was swamped. But the passengers fought off the Indians and managed to get the boat bailed out and afloat once more. Among those fighting and bailing was Mrs. Ephraim Peyton, who had given birth to a son the day before. Unfortunately, the infant was lost overboard during the confusion. Another boat had been captured by the Chickamaugas, and all those aboard had been killed on the spot.

Such was Charlotte Robertson's introduction to Indian fighting on the Tennessee River. Now, a year later, she watched as her husband and several other men armed themselves and mounted their horses to pursue the three Indians who had just fired at the fort on the bluff above the Cumberland. The warriors were Chickamaugas led by Dragging Canoe. Having failed to stop the settlers from penetrating his territory, he had come to wipe out their village. As her husband led the men from the stockade, Charlotte climbed to the walkway that allowed defenders to see over the palisade. Something in the treeline along a creek caught her attention. She began to call to the men and to wave her apron to attract their attention, but with no success. The men rode on. The Indians stopped at the edge of the woods not far from the fort, and the pursuit force from the stockade dismounted as soon as they got within gunshot range. Just then, a large party of Indians came rushing out of their hiding place in the bed of a creek. The men led by Robertson had been ambushed. Other Indians came charging out of a cedar thicket and moved toward the fort, cutting off Robertson and his companions from their route of escape.

All the noise and confusion stampeded the horses the men had ridden out from the fort. The loss of the horses was a serious matter because the animals pulled plows as well as provided transportation, but the men were more concerned at the moment with losing their lives. The horses were such a valuable prize that many of the Indians broke off the attack to chase them.

Charlotte Robertson, from her vantage point on the stockade walkway, could see the breaks in the Indian ranks as the warriors went after the horses. Running down to the entrance of the fort, Charlotte opened the gate and then turned and opened the door to the dogs' pen. This was the fort's secret weapon: more than fifty large dogs, many of them a crossbreed with English mastiffs, trained to attack.

The Cherokees, like all Eastern Woodland Indians, kept dogs as companions around the village and on the hunt. But these attack dogs were huge brutes and not easily beaten off or killed. Soon, the field around the fort was a swirling mass of horses, Indians, and dogs. Robertson led his party through the mele to regain the fort.

By mid-morning Dragging Canoe and his war party had had enough, and they faded away into the surrounding woods. However, the battle was not over for Charlotte. She began to help care for the wounded, among whom was her son Felix. He had been knocked down and scalped while still alive. Charlotte held her son's head in her lap while one of the men jabbed a large needle into the lad's skull. A secretion flowed from the punctures and formed a crust, allowing the wound to heal eventually. Charlotte Robertson, by her actions, had helped to secure the fort and overcome the Indians in the "Battle of the Bluffs."

Roman Legionnaires Aid the Patriots

On the South Carolina frontier in the early spring of 1781 at Wrights Bluff, the ghosts of Roman legionnaires arose from their distant graves to assist the Patriot forces commanded by Col. Henry "Light Horse Harry" Lee and Gen. Francis Marion. From the mists of the past, the skills and techniques of these long-dead soldiers made possible a victory over the British.

In the broad strategic picture, the British success in the southern colonies was withering away. Lord Cornwallis was leading the main British army northward into Virginia along a road that would lead, eventually, to Yorktown and a climactic Patriot victory. Behind Cornwallis, leaders such as Nathanael Greene, Henry Lee, Thomas Sumter, and Francis Marion were isolating and wiping out the fortified positions that had been established by the Royal Army in an attempt to control the countryside.

Francis Marion had already become famous as a leader of irregular troops, fighting what later generations would call a guerrilla war, although that term was not in usage among English-speaking people during the Revolutionary War. Because of his success, Col. Henry Lee and a group of regular troops, the Continentals, had been sent to join Marion to provide the firepower and disciplined strike force the guerrillas often lacked. On April 14, 1781, these two Patriot leaders met and decided that the next target in the campaign to retake the South would be the British position at Fort Watson.

The location for Fort Watson had been carefully chosen. In an area of flat terrain, the British had found an Indian burial mound some 30 feet in height. A stockade built of heavy logs was erected atop the mound, and three lines of abatis were stretched around its bottom. The abatis were built of treetops, with the branches tangled together and the ends trimmed into sharp points facing the direction from which any enemy would approach. These barriers were the equivalent of today's barbed wire entanglements. All trees and bushes had been cleared for 200 yards around the fort so the defenders would have a clear field of fire, and so there would be no cover for an attacker. The weak point of the defenses was that water had to be brought from a lake several hundred yards beyond the walls. Inside this strong position were 120 men, regulars and militia combined, under the command of Lt. James McKay.

It was an easy task for Marion and Lee to surround the fort and to station sharpshooters to pick off any of the garrison trying to go to the lake for water. Lieutenant McKay was not going to give up that easily, however, and put his men to digging a well. Meanwhile, each side took occasional long-range shots at each other. On April 18, just as the last kegs of water in the fort were being tapped, the diggers struck water. Now, it appeared the fort might hold out indefinitely.

Marion and Lee were worried. They did not have the entrenching tools at hand to undertake a formal siege. That time-consuming method required digging a trench parallel to the enemy position to protect one's own men, then digging a zigzag approach, or "sap," to get closer to the enemy, followed by another parallel, and so on until the trenches were close enough to allow troops to charge the walls. Not only did the Patriots lack entrenching tools, they lacked time. The British were gathering the garrisons from other fortified positions and were preparing to attack Marion and Lee from the rear.

If only they had a cannon, Lee thought. Even a small piece of artillery would make short work of the wooden stockade. So a messenger on a good horse was sent to the main Patriot army to ask for a cannon, but it was doubtful that artillery could be moved fast enough over the wretched roads to arrive in time to capture the fort before a British rescue force would arrive.

Then an even greater threat appeared. A few men in the Patriot camp came down with smallpox. Given the crowded conditions under which the men lived, this disease could sweep through the entire force in a flash. Lee's regulars had been inoculated, but few of Marion's militia had been. These guerrilla fighters did not fear the British, but the thought of catching smallpox unnerved them. Every night men slipped away from the camp.

The fear of disease and the worry of an attack from the rear were made worse by the men having nothing to do. The troops needed to be kept busy, and there needed to be some progress toward capturing the fort if morale was to be maintained.

Among the besiegers was Lt. Col. Hezikiah Maham of the St. Stephen's Parish militia. Maham had seen quite a bit of war, having served as a captain in a rifle regiment before accepting his commission as an officer in the militia cavalry. As he led his men on patrols through the surrounding countryside, watching for the approach of a British relief force, Lieutenant Colonel Maham pondered the problem of how to capture the fort. His mind wandered back to his school days when he had studied Latin and had translated *Caesar's Commentaries* about Roman military actions in Gaul. The Roman soldiers he had read about often came up against fortifications, and they certainly had no artillery. How had they captured forts? Then he remembered. Siege towers.

The Roman legionnaires built wooden towers taller than the walls they were attacking. These towers were mounted on wheels and were pushed up close to the walls, a ramp was lowered, and soldiers charged across to capture the fort. The concept would have to be modified, Maham knew, but the Patriots had axes, and the militiamen were accustomed to using them every day on their farms.

Maham took his plan to Marion and Lee, and the two immediately endorsed it. Soon, details of men were going into the nearby woods, and axes were crashing into the trunks of trees. The British garrison could hear the sound of chopping, but the Patriots carefully kept all their preparations out of sight. For five days teams of men cut logs to specific lengths, while other teams cut notches near each end of each log. On the night of April 22, shielded by darkness, the prefabricated pieces were carried to within easy rifle range of the fort, and a square crib of logs was raised. When the tower wall was tall enough to allow a marksman to see into the interior of the fort, a floor was laid. Then a parapet of logs was built on the side next to the fort. Before daylight, riflemen were atop the tower, waiting for a target.

Lt. James McKay had been warned by sentries that there was a lot of noise coming from the Patriot camp, so he had all his men at their battle positions on the walls ready to repel a dawn attack. The growing light revealed a tower, nearly 45 feet high, looming over his men. From the top of the tower, rifles began to crack, and McKay's men began to fall. Quickly, he ordered the garrison under cover, but as soon as the British were off the walls, parties of axe men rushed from the Patriot lines to hew lanes through the abatis. In a short while axes were thudding against the logs of the palisade, while the Continental troops fell into formation with bayonets fixed, ready to charge into the first gap to open. Reluctantly, Lieutenant McKay lowered the Union Jack. And somewhere the shade of Julius Caesar surely smiled. His legions had won yet another victory.

Worms Won the War for the Patriots

When Lord Cornwallis handed over his sword in surrender at Yorktown, Virginia, on September 19, 1781, the climactic moment of the Revolution had been reached. Although the war would not end for another two years, the surrender at Yorktown convinced the British government to begin negotiations that would recognize American independence.

Lord Cornwallis did not surrender because he had been outmaneuverered or outgeneraled. Cornwallis had deliberately chosen his position at Yorktown and had entrenched there by choice. His reason for choosing that position was his expectation that the Royal Navy would come to the river port and embark his force to convey it to New York City. The capitulation of the British army was the result of the defeat of the Royal Navy in an engagement at the mouth of Chesapeake Bay. At this decisive battle no Americans were present. The French fleet under Adm. Francois DeGrasse confronted the British fleet under Rear Adm. Thomas Graves. But the Americans had a powerful ally native to their shores—a tiny, wood-boring worm that had attacked the hulls of many British vessels. The practice of covering the hulls of ships below the waterline with sheets of copper to protect them against worms had begun by this time, but the French had added this feature to more of their ships than the British had. Several of the British battleships still had unprotected wooden bottoms, and in the warm waters of the Caribbean and southern American coast, these soon became infested with worms.

During the summer of 1781, the French steadily dispatched elements of their navy to protect their possessions in the Caribbean and to support their American allies. A key component of this support was a fleet of twenty-eight battleships, called ships of the line, which included the *Ville de Paris*. This latter ship mounted one hundred cannons and was considered to be the most powerful ship afloat.

The British maintained a large fleet in American waters and sent even more ships during the summer of 1781 to maintain their numerical superiority. As the summer progressed and the hurricane season approached, both fleets began to move north to safer waters. The British thought Admiral DeGrasse would send only twelve to fifteen battleships north and decided to send a slightly larger number themselves. The French were known to have eight battleships at Newport, Rhode Island. If DeGrasse sent fifteen of his ships north, there would be a total French fleet of twenty-three battleships on the American coast. The British had seven battleships at New York City and three at other American locations. They planned to reinforce these with twenty-one from the Caribbean, thus having an advantage of thirty-one to twenty-three ships present.

From the beginning of the move, the Patriot's secret ally, the wood worm, made its presence known. Seven of the British ships scheduled for deployment to New York were found to be so badly worm-eaten that they were judged to be unfit for further duty. These seven mounted a total of 436 cannons. This left only fourteen battleships to reinforce those already in North American waters.

Under the command of Admiral Hood, these ships sailed north and east along the American coast. On reaching New York City, another unpleasant fact had to be confronted. Rear Admiral Graves had two ships away on other duty. This left only five ships to join with Hood. The other three British battleships in American waters were likewise occupied. The projected British concentration of thirty-one ships had shrunk to nineteen.

By this time Admiral Hood knew he was needed in the Chesapeake to join with Lord Cornwallis. He also made the reasonable assumption that Admiral DeGrasse would have the same location as his objective. But the worms were still at work. Almost as soon as the nineteen battleships had left New York City, the *Terrible* had to signal a request that the fleet halt so repairs could be made. The bottom of *Terrible* had become so leaky due to worms that she had to have five pumps going constantly. As temporary repairs were made to *Terrible,* an inspection revealed that *Ajax, Montague,* and *Europe* were in almost as bad a condition.

DeGrasse was indeed waiting for Hood, but not in the most advantageous position. The French ships were anchored inside the mouth of Chesapeake Bay, dispersed in three lines so they blockaded both the James and the York Rivers. The fleet was also weakened by having 1,500 men absent in the ships' boats taking water and supplies to the Patriot and French armies besieging Yorktown. However, DeGrasse commanded twenty-seven ships mounting more than 2,000 cannons, while the British had only nineteen ships carrying 1,500 big guns. Had it not been for the British ships sent home because of worm damage, the strength in ships and guns would have been equal.

On September 5, 1781, the British approached the entrance to Chesapeake Bay and caught sight of the French fleet. Almost at the same time, the French began preparations to leave their anchorage and to sail out against their enemy. The French were at some disadvantage because the wind and the tide were in their faces, while the British had both behind them. In trying to get out of the confined spaces of the bay's mouth, the French ships became somewhat scattered.

The British now had an excellent opportunity to use the advantage of wind and tide to make up for their smaller numbers by attacking before the French were ready. Instead, the British placed the leaky *Terrible* in the lead of their line and slowly worked their way into position. It took six hours for the fleets to get in position to open the battle.

The French practice in battle was to fire primarily at the masts and rigging of opposing ships, attempting to cripple the enemy. Damaged ships could be finished off at leisure once the main battle was over. The British, however, favored firing at the hull of an opponent in an attempt to sink the enemy on the spot. In this engagement the French method proved to be superior, and soon the rigging of the British ships were cut up, slowing their speed. Those shots that missed the rigging took effect in the hulls of the British ships, hulls weakened by worms in many cases, and soon several ships were taking on water faster than crews could pump it out.

Darkness put an end to the firing, and both sides began to make temporary repairs. The British found the task impossible in some cases, and one ship, the *Terrible*, was allowed to go to the bottom of the sea, while others attempted to limp away toward New York City. When dawn came, the French were ready to renew the battle, but the British found it necessary to retire.

The French seamen had fought bravely and well. Their victory would lead to the beginning of the end of the war and independence for a new nation. No Americans were present at the Battle of the Chesapeake, but a very capable ally was, the tiny wood-boring worm that so ably helped the Patriot cause.

A Potpourri of Revolutionary War Facts

• Had Britain not won the Seven Years' War, there might have been no American Revolution. It was taxes imposed to pay the cost of that victory that stirred Americans to resistance and then to independence.

• Samuel Adams, who led opposition to Royal taxes in Boston, was a former tax collector.

• One son of Benjamin Franklin supported the Crown during the Revolution.

• At the time of the Revolution, Paul Revere was better known as an engraver and silversmith than as a messenger for the Patriot cause. His fame as a messenger was established by a poem written in 1876.

• During the Revolution approximately 20 percent of the American population were Tories who supported Britain; 20 percent were neutral toward the war; 20 percent were slaves whom the British offered freedom. Only about 40 percent of the population actively supported the cause of independence.

• Antoine Laurent Lavoisier never set foot in America, but his work for the French government produced a formula for a superior type of gunpowder that helped America win the war.

• The largest army ever commanded by George Washington was one of about twenty-six thousand men.

• Baron von Steuben, the famous Prussian soldier who supported the Patriot cause, was not a baron at all. He had no title of nobility and had not held a military command for fourteen years before coming to America.

• Expelled from the capitol in Williamsburg by the Royal governor, the Virginia House of Burgesses met for a time in Raleigh Tavern.

• The British general Thomas Gage was born in America, as was his wife.

• The first Patriot generals are today virtually unknown. They were Jedediah Preble, Artemas Ward, Seth Pomeroy, John Thomas, and William Heath.

• The warning spread on the night before Lexington and Concord was, "The Redcoats are coming." To have said "The British are coming" would have made no sense because everyone in the colonies was considered British.

• The grandfather of novelist Herman Melville, author of *Moby Dick,* participated in the Boston Tea Party.

• In June 1775 the British warship HMS *Margaretta* was boarded and captured by a group of Patriots armed largely with axes and pitchforks.

• It was Gen. Henry "Light Horse Harry" Lee who said of Washington that he was "first in war, first in peace, and first in the hearts of his countrymen."

• King George III paid seven pounds for each German mercenary he hired and promised the ruler of the German states from which the man came an additional seven pounds if the man was killed.

• Many Patriot cavalrymen had their sabers made by local blacksmiths who used steel from saws taken from sawmills.

• The war had been in progress for eighteen months before the first flag with "stars and stripes" was adopted by the Patriot forces.

• A British soldier had to complete seventeen distinct steps to load and fire one shot from his musket.

• The Rev. Mr. Peter Muhlenburg rose in the pulpit of his Woodstock, Virginia, church to preach one Sunday in 1776. Taking as his text, "To everything there is a season," the parson delivered a fiery sermon, then threw off his clerical robe and stood before the congregation dressed in the uniform of a Patriot officer. Instead of calling on sinners to repent, he called on men to enlist.

• "Molly Pitcher," who nursed soldiers and fought in the Battle of Monmouth, is the most legendary of them, but many women accompanied their husbands into battle.

• Col. Laommi Baldwin of the twenty-sixth Massachusetts Infantry was the horticulturalist who developed the Baldwin apple. For nearly 150 years this was the most widely grown of all American apples.

• One of George Washington's bodyguards, Thomas Hickey, plotted with the British to kidnap Washington. The plot was discovered, and Hickey became the first American soldier to be executed.

• Patriots in New York City toppled a statue of King George III and melted the metal to mold over 42,000 bullets to be fired at the King's soldiers.

• Only forty-nine U.S. Marines were killed during the entire war.

• Henry Dawkins was arrested in 1776 for making counterfeit American money. However, his copies were so much better than the originals that Congress hired Dawkins to make the real thing for them.

• There is no firm historical evidence as to who designed the U.S. flag.

• Christopher Ludwick of Philadelphia frequently infiltrated the British lines to urge German mercenaries to desert and become farmers in Pennsylvania. Many did.

• What is known as the Battle of Bunker Hill was actually fought on Breed's Hill. The Patriots intended to take Bunker Hill as well, but the British attacked before they could.

• Late in 1776 some of George Washington's men captured a pet dog belonging to the British commander Sir William Howe. Washington had the dog returned.

• Henry Laurens of South Carolina was captured by the British while traveling to Holland as an ambassador for the Patriot cause. He was imprisoned in the Tower of London for several months. After the surrender of the British army at Yorktown, Virginia, in 1781, Laurens was exchanged for Lord Cornwallis, the commander of the surrendered army.

Bibliography

Alden, John Richard. *The American Revolution.* New York: Harper Colopon Books, 1954.

AmericanRevolution.Org (www.americanrevolution.org).

Babits, Lawrence E. *A Devil of a Whipping: The Battle of Cowpens.* Chapel Hill: University of North Carolina Press, 1998.

Bass, Robert D. *The Green Dragoon.* Columbia, SC: Sandlapper Press, 1973.

Commager, Henry Steele, and Richard B. Morris. *The Spirit of Seventy-Six.* New York: Harper and Row, 1958.

Dupuy, R. Ernest, and Trevor N. Dupuy. *The Compact History of the Revolutionary War.* New York: Hawthorne Books, 1963.

Dykeman, Wilma. *The Battle of Kings Mountain: With Fire and Sword.* Washington, DC: National Park Service, 1991.

Evans, Emory G. *Thomas Nelson of Yorktown: Revolutionary Virginian.* Williamsburg, VA: The Colonial Williamsburg Foundation, 1975.

Fast, Howard. *The Crossing.* New York: William Morrow & Company, 1971,

Fleming, Thomas. *1776: Year of Illusions.* New York: W. W. Norton & Company, 1975.

Garrison, Webb. *Sidelights on the American Revolution.* Nashville, TN: Abingdon Press, 1974.

Hawke, David F. *Honorable Treason: The Declaration of Independence and the Men Who Signed It.* New York: Viking Press, 1976.

Ketchum, Richard M. *Saratoga: Turning Point of America's Revolutionary War.* New York: Henry Holt and Company, 1997.

———. *The Winter Soldiers.* New York: Anchor Books, 1975.

Lancaster, Bruce, and J. H. Plumb. *Book of the Revolution.* New York: Dell Publishing, 1958.

Larrabee, Harold A. *Decision at the Chesapeake.* London: William Kimber, 1964.

Lengyel, Cornel. *Four Days in July: The Story Behind the Declaration of Independence.* New York: Bantam Books. 1958.

McCants, E. C. *History, Stories and Legends of South Carolina.* Dallas, TX: Southern Publishing Company, 1927.

Morrison, Samuel Eliot. *John Paul Jones: A Sailor's Biography.* Boston: Little, Brown, & Company, 1959.

Murray, Stuart. *America's Song: The Story of "Yankee Doodle."* Bennington, VT: Images from the Past, 1999.

Pearson, Michael. *The Revolutionary War.* New York: Capricorn Books, 1972.

Quarles, Benjamin. *The Negro in the American Revolution.* Chapel Hill: University of North Carolina Press, 1961.

Stohlman, Martha Lou Lemmon. *John Witherspoon: Parson, Politician, Patriot.* Philadelphia, PA: The Westminster Press, 1976.

Wood, W. J. *Battles of the Revolutionary War.* New York: De Capo Press, 1990.

Zobel, Hiller B. *The Boston Massacre.* New York: W. W. Norton & Company, 1970.

Index

F

G

H

I

J

K

Y

About the Author

Michael R. Bradley received a Ph.D. in History from Vanderbilt University in 1970 and has taught at Motlow College in Lynchburg, Tennessee, since that time. He is the author of several collections of true Civil War stories, including *Old Times There Are Not Forgotten*, *To Live and Die in Dixie*, *Early on a Frosty Morn*, and *Land of Cotton*. Dr. Bradley has also written a history of an overlooked Civil War campaign, *Tullahoma: The 1863 Campaign for Control of Middle Tennessee*. He is the author of Globe Pequot Press's *It Happened in the Civil War*. Dr. Bradley frequently leads tours of historic sites in Middle Tennessee.

NOTES

NOTES

NOTES

NOTES

NOTES

NOTES

NOTES

NOTES

NOTES